How to

Read

(and Write About)

Poetry

How to Read (and Write About) Poetry

(and Write About)

Poetry

Susan Holbrook

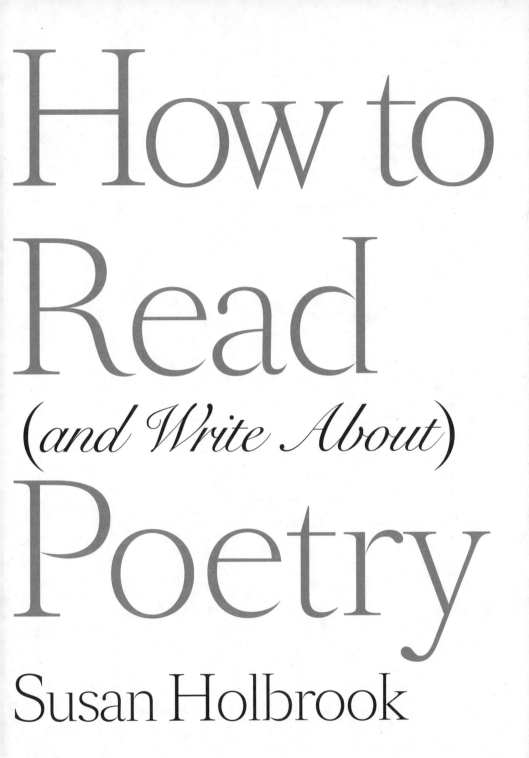

broadview press

Library and Archives Canada Cataloguing in Publication

Holbrook, Susan L. (Susan Leslie), 1967-, author
How to read (and write about) poetry / Susan Holbrook.

Includes bibliographical references and index.
ISBN 978-1-55111-991-5 (paperback)

1. Poetry—Explication. 2. English poetry—History and criticism. 3. American poetry—History and criticism. 4. Canadian poetry (English)—History and criticism. I. Title.

PN1031.H64 2015   808.1   C2015-902438-2

Broadview Press is an independent, international publishing house, incorporated in 1985.

We welcome comments and suggestions regarding any aspect of our publications—please feel free to contact us at the addresses below or at broadview@broadviewpress.com.

North America:
PO Box 1243, Peterborough, Ontario K9J 7H5, Canada
555 Riverwalk Parkway, Tonawanda, NY 14150, USA
Tel: (705) 743–8990; Fax: (705) 743–8353
Email: customerservice@broadviewpress.com

UK, Europe, Central Asia, Middle East, Africa, India, and Southeast Asia:
Eurospan Group, 3 Henrietta St., London WC2E 8LU, UK
Tel: 44 (0) 1767 604972; Fax: 44 (0) 1767 601640
Email: eurospan@turpin-distribution.com

Australia and New Zealand:
Footprint Books
1/6a Prosperity Parade, Warriewood, NSW 2102, Australia
Tel: 61 1300 260 090; Fax: 61 02 9997 3185
email: info@footprint.com.au

www.broadviewpress.com

Broadview Press acknowledges the financial support of the Government of Canada through the Canada Book Fund for our publishing activities.

Edited by Michel Pharand

Book design and composition by George Kirkpatrick
PRINTED IN CANADA

Poetry is always unbearable
in terms of the tension it creates
in meaning.

—Nicole Brossard

I was always shy about "poetry."
I didn't know quite what it was.
And I think I was right to be shy
of it, because nobody quite knows
what it is. I'm still not sure.

—Seamus Heaney

Contents

Acknowledgements

FIRST, HEARTFELT THANKS TO Broadview Press for patience, indulgence, and guidance over the years it's taken me to compose this book. Thanks especially to Marjorie Mather for wise, attentive shepherding and Michel Pharand, Tara Trueman, and Judith Earnshaw for invaluable edits. I am grateful to Julia Gaunce, past editor at Broadview, for early discussions of the project.

Where would anybody be without librarians? My thanks to Brian Owens and Ana-Maria Staffen, who work in Rare Books and Special Collections at the Leddy Library, University of Windsor. Deep gratitude to Heidi Jacobs, Information Literacy Librarian at Leddy, for editorial suggestions, invaluable expertise, and general great chumminess.

My brilliant colleagues in the English department at the University of Windsor have been steadfast sources of information and inspiration. To Nicole Markotic, Thomas Dilworth, and Louis Cabri I extend appreciation for our life-long conversations about all things poetry.

Love and thanks to my partner, Lori, and daughter, Elise, for keeping things quiet on weekend mornings so I could work on the book; and thanks also for doing the opposite—the singing and playing I heard through the office wall reminded me of the inextricable kinship between music and poetry.

My biggest thanks must go to all the students I've had in the past couple of decades. Your insightfulness and enthusiasm knock me out. But I was equally propelled, in the writing of this book, by your frustration and bewilderment. Thanks for all those questions you prefaced with phrases such as "I don't know anything about poetry, but ...," "This is a really stupid question, but ...," and "Poetry is not my favourite, so...." I hope this book supplies some answers, and some further questions, which foster your confidence and desire to study poetry.

How to Use This Book

THIS BOOK IS AN invitation and initiation into the exciting, challenging, inspiring, puzzling, energizing, weird world of poetry. I wrote it after a couple of decades teaching in undergraduate literature classrooms, where I noticed the genre of poetry invariably triggered unease.

I want, in this book, to get conversations going about poetry, and to involve you in those conversations. Most of the book is comprised of chapters in which I discuss a meaty poem, and introduce questions, literary terms and reading strategies with an eye to building up your own critical abilities. A word in capital letters flags it as an important poetic term that is fully defined in the *Glossary of Poetic Terms* at the back of the book. At the end of each of these discussion chapters you'll find a short gathering of poems to which you can bring some of the new skills you've acquired.

Dispersed among these chapters are several Research Tips, designed to familiarize you with methods of secondary research. These tips will help you locate and navigate critical, historical, biographical, and cultural resources that can enrich your engagement with a poem. Many resources are available in both print and online versions. Some online resources are open access (that is, anybody can read them); where online resources demand subscription, students may have access through their institution's library site.

You can either consult the *Brief Guide to Meter* as needed, or discover the art of scansion before taking on the discussion chapters. Understanding the sonic features of a work is key to exploring its energies and effects and, in many poems, meter is a key component of that soundscape.

Finally, the book offers guidance on *How to Write about Poetry*. After reading the first ten chapters, you'll be primed to generate all kinds of original observations and insights about any poem you encounter. An essay is really just a carefully orchestrated and focussed presentation of such unique readings. Consult this chapter for advice on the preparation, planning, composition, and formatting of a compelling essay that contributes to the field of poetic criticism.

In addition to providing definitions for all the literary terms introduced in this book, the *Glossary of Poetic Terms* includes terms not engaged here, so that it might continue to serve as a useful resource as you proceed with your studies of poetry.

(A note on dates: I supply dates to locate the works in their cultural context. Dates indicate the year of first publication in a book or major periodical.)

Introduction: What Makes Poetry Poetry and Why Are We So Afraid of It?

"AVANT-GARDE TOILET PAPER," I hear a student mutter as this poem by the Canadian poet bp Nichol (1944–88) flashes up on the screen. My "Writing About Literature" class has just spent a month happily and gamely discussing short stories, but on the day we are to start the poetry unit, the mood has changed. Why is this poem immediately dismissed as flushable? Why does everybody look so anxious? What's so scary about poetry?

I put the question to my students, ask them why they think so many people get nervous about poetry. Here are a few of their answers: "There are so many hidden meanings." "Sometimes I feel like the author is tricking me." "Writers never just come out and say what they mean." "There's no one clear meaning." For these students, prose is a more reliable communicator. They know how to read the sentences and get meaning from them.

Poetic language, apparently, is getting in the way.

How does poetic language differ from the language of prose? You are probably already familiar with a number of features of poetic language, and know how to name them, using terms such as ALLITERATION, METAPHOR, CHIASMUS (if you don't know that last one, you soon will—it's a fun one!). In truth, such deviations from bald declarative prose characterize all literary language, whether in poetry, fiction or drama. Poetry, however, lies at the far end of the spectrum, rich with language that doesn't behave in familiar ways.

In daily life we encounter lots of language that aims to communicate something to us unambiguously: explanations in textbooks, news articles, medication instructions, product user guides. We don't even notice language in these cases; we consume the messages as if the language were a transparent window onto what we want to know. Continuing with this analogy, we can think of poetic language as a kind of stained glass window. It's not a swift and invisible portal to meaning. It's now an object in itself that we have become aware of, and as we look at it from different angles, and look through the different colours of glass, what we see through it shifts. The meaning is not simply out there, "hidden" by the coloured glass. Instead, meaning is shaped in multiple ways by its medium.

One of the ways most poetry differs from prose is through LINEATION. While the right hand margin determines where this line of type will end, poets make conscious choices about where to terminate lines. In prose, the primary unit of composition is the sentence, its placement on the page of no consequence. In poetry, the principal unit is the line, so that placement of words on the page, the organization of words and space, is significant. The shape of a poem, like the stained glass window, is visible and contributes to meaning. If the lineation of poetry begins to move us into an awareness of language as visible material on the page, bp Nichol's poem above insists on that awareness, its success dependent on our willingness to pay attention to how his letters are oriented in space. If we trace the word "poet" to its roots, we find the Greek *poeien* (to make), and further back the Indo European *kwei* (to pile up, to build). Nichol's work reminds us that a poem is a made thing, an object composed of the stuff of language. The piled up letters are making meaning, not hiding it; they are the way of meaning, not in its way. Nichol's poem, entitled "Blues," is an example of CONCRETE POETRY, a genre of poetry that foregrounds the material resources (visual and aural) of language. I start with this poem because it illustrates so clearly what makes poetry poetry; in poetic language, form matters and is inextricably entwined with content.

Let's read Nichol's poem. At that prospect a student nervous about poetry might be balking already. Clearly "reading" this poem will not be anything like "reading" a story. The American poet Charles Bernstein offers this advice to anxious poetry readers: "Don't let the poem intimidate you! Often the difficult poem will provoke you, but this may be its way of getting your attention" (5). The first thing we can do, then, is relax and try to reshape our emotional response to the unfamiliarity of the text. If a poem "provokes," if it is provocative to us, that could mean it irritates, challenges us; but we could also see the provocative poem as enticing, stimulating. It's all right to enter some unknown territory, to read something you don't know how to read; when it comes to poetry, nobody has all-encompassing mastery. In the end you'll find that the oddities, the questions, the ambiguities, the surprises, the provocations are the very qualities of poetry that enable you to enjoy a lifelong relationship with it. So, "Blues" has our attention. Now what?

The first thing we might do is look at the poem as an object. bp Nichol was interested in blurring boundaries between the arts. The arrangement of letters and words in this work invites us to move beyond our habitual left-to-right reading strategy and engage it as we would visual art. Looking at the poem for a while reveals its symmetry: the diagonal row of e's acts as a mirror, an axis of reflection. The reflected image is composed of the letters l, o, and v, presented in a font that highlights their elemental shapes (circle, line, chevron) and renders each of them symmetrical. One way to look at the overall shape is as two arrows meeting in the middle of that central square. At the same time that our eyes are registering these visual patterns, we can't help but read the word "love." A cluster of ideas and associations—love, Cupid's arrows, mirroring—begins to accrue as we build meaning in this poem.

Because of the symmetry of the poem, the 'word' that appears as often as "love," both horizontally and vertically, is "evol." What is "evol"? Perhaps it is a word fragment, the beginning of 'evolve'; love is, after all, the engine of evolution! But we can also sound out "evol" and hear 'evil,' remembering that the title of the poem is "Blues." The musical genre of Blues gives us compelling songs infused with lament, often about the dark side of love. The musical title encourages us to think further about the sounds in this poem. The "oooo"s and the "eeeeeee" might express the pleasure of love, the pain of love or, as we hear so often in Blues music, both.

You might find yourself constructing a little narrative out of this constellation of letters: somebody has perhaps been jilted by a lover, and is eeeeeing and oooooing over lost delights. It's interesting that we so often gravitate toward story, even when considering a poem such as "Blues," which looks nothing like a story. Remember my students, who had no trouble tackling the fiction unit of my class. Some theorists have suggested that a storytelling drive has evolved in humans, so that we tend to communicate, express ourselves, and even think in a narrative mode. Jonathan Gottschall argues that we think in stories because it "allows us to experience our lives as coherent, orderly and meaningful. It is what makes life more than blooming, buzzing confusion" (102). So why not declare that the "hidden meaning" of "Blues" is a tale of thwarted passion? Or why not translate the poem into a simple sentence, such as 'Love has its ups and downs' or, to pursue another interpretation, 'One person's love is another person's evil'? We might even note the name "eve" in there, evoking the familiar biblical tale of Eve's discovery of evil in the garden of Eden. But although poetry often features elements of story—the most famous early poems in Western culture, the *Iliad* and the *Odyssey*, are narrative—if we invoke again the idea of a spectrum of literary language, poetry lies at one end, working in all kinds of modes other than story. Our engagement with "Blues," for example, deals with shape, sound, mood, patterns, associations. The poem is full of "blooming" and "buzzing" that confounds and delights and invites you to look and listen.

The meanings are piling up. "Poetry is always unbearable in terms of the tension it creates in meaning" (10). So says the famous Québécoise poet Nicole Brossard. Given that she has published dozens of books, the "unbearable" for her must be a positive; the multiplicity and ambiguity of meaning in poetry is not to be borne lightly, because it is formidable, explosive, inexhaustible. We shouldn't feel pressure to reduce the poem to a simple summarizing sentence because it really can't be done. Not only would such a statement exclude alternate meanings, but to attempt it would be to commit what is called the HERESY OF PARAPHRASE. This term was coined by mid-century literary critic Cleanth Brooks, who argued that a poem is an experience, like music or dance; the unique features of poetic language, the form of the poem, constitute its power. There's no putting a poem in a nutshell.

We are accustomed to moving our eyes left to right as we consume written material, leaving words behind once we've read them. "Blues" compels our eyes to move diagonally, back and forth, up and down, near and far; there are all manner of ways to take in and make sense of the patterns. By keeping our eyes active on the page, the poem inspires a kind of meditation. It's a meditation on love, but also on language itself. That is, we do not normally interact so intimately with the letters of our alphabet; the result is that we begin to look at something familiar as if we've never encountered it before. l, o, v, and e are suddenly like characters in a foreign language, their physical contours apparent to us. The letters might seem imbued with the magic they carried when we first learned them as children. "Blues" sparks up the relationship with language that started when we were in diapers. But why should your relationship with the letter e matter?

The eighteenth-century poet Alexander Pope argued that poetic language gives us "What oft was Thought, but ne'er so well Exprest" (298); his view was that ideally poetry can communicate with unprecedented vividness the contents of our minds. The Romantic poets went further, suggesting that poetic language could actually create new thought, bring about original ideas. In his essay "A Defence of Poetry," the Romantic poet Percy Bysshe Shelley calls poetry "the root and blossom of all other systems of thought" (38), a force which can produce "forms of opinion and action never before conceived" (25). It's this notion that language creates knowledge and shapes worldviews that points to the reason your relationship with the letter e matters.

Since linguistic anthropologist Benjamin Lee Whorf proposed, in the early twentieth century, that the differences among cultures were in part determined by their respective languages, there has been an active conversation about how languages might shape our realities. If you speak more than one language, you might already be familiar with the sensation of having a slightly different worldview, feeling like a slightly different person, depending on which idiom you're using. More than a millennium before the SAPIR-WHORF HYPOTHESIS, the medieval ruler Charlemagne noted that, "to have a second language is to have a second soul." If language contours the way we think, then, all the language coming at you every day—advertising, news broadcasts, articles, books—is shaping who you are and how you see the world. If poetry can ignite an awareness of letters and words in you, a more active relationship with this powerful stuff that is language, then perhaps you can be more conscious about that shaping, become a more critical thinker about your world as you participate in it as a citizen. One of bp Nichol's fellow concrete poets, Bill Bissett, said of their practice, "We really believed if we freed the word we could help free people" (*bp: pushing*). This philosophy recalls Shelley's famous claim that "poets are the unacknowledged legislators of the world" ("Defence" 46). Thanks to avant-garde toilet paper, you might see and hear more acutely the cultural messages (for example, about "love" and "evil") affecting your life, and you might even feel empowered to intervene in the words/worlds around you.

So, in addition to offering aesthetic delight and windows on (not to mention contributions to) history, philosophy, culture, etc., poetry can change the world—not a bad reason to stick with it. Oddly, sometimes you'll hear critics say that concrete poetry, the genre that facilitates the most intimate connection between you and your language, is not really poetry at all. The *Oxford Dictionary of Literary Terms* claims that most concrete poems "have little claim to the status of poetry" (67). You might also hear that PROSE POEMS, poems made of sentences and often dispensing with lineation, don't qualify. The prose poem has gained increasing prominence over the last century, and masterworks of the genre have been produced by poets such as Gertrude Stein, Allen Ginsberg, Lyn Hejinian, Daphne Marlatt, Fred Wah, Anne Carson, and Ron Silliman. Yet some critics will say, "the very notion of a 'prose poem' is oxymoronic" (Furniss and Bath 64). (An OXYMORON, by the way, is a figure of speech which links irreconcilable parts, or contradictory terms, such as 'cold sun'). I'm with the poets on this one. If bp Nichol says it's a poem, let's call it a poem. And if Nobel-prize laureate Seamus Heaney says, as he does in the epigraph to this book, that he's "still not sure" what poetry is, I'm not about to insist on any fast definitions.

You probably have this book in your hand because poetry is such a mysterious, fugitive, shifting, befuddling, multifaceted, and indefinable thing. Reading *How to Read (and Write About) Poetry* won't evacuate poetry of its complexity, but I hope the book will change how you feel about that complexity. Through discussion of a number of great poems from various periods, this book will introduce you to literary terms, genres, poetic movements, cultural histories, reading strategies, etc., not with an aim to grant you mastery over the unmasterable, but to equip you to join the ongoing critical conversations about poetry.

I'd like to end this introduction with a final attempt to jettison the idea of "hidden meanings" by talking about where meaning is. There's even a diagram.

Students often think of meaning as residing in the mind of the author; if only we could raise Gertrude Stein from the dead, we could find out what she really meant by "Rose is a rose is a rose"! The problem with authors is, as any interview with an author will show, they themselves keep changing their minds about poems. Writers grow and evolve, and develop new relationships with the words appearing in their work. Even if you could interview the author as he or she was writing the poem, neither you nor that author would have access to the subconscious forces contributing to the creative project. When it comes to poems written by "Anonymous," we don't have a hope of getting information from the source; yet such poems don't lack meaning. It's interesting to hear what authors have to say about their compositional methods, and about what a work means to them, but it's only one piece of the puzzle.

You are the most important piece. How you respond to the tensions and music and images and themes of a poem will constitute the heart of any analysis you offer. If you've ever taken part in a class discussion of a poem, you know that there will be as many readings of it as there are individuals in the room. Your reception of the language is active, is meaning-making, just as the author's production of it was. What's more, with your historical hindsight, you will be able to note forces at work in a poem that authors from the past, steeped in their own culture, may not even have been fully conscious of. And your unique life experiences (all you've read, thought, seen, learned, felt) ensure that the chord struck between you and the poem will be unique, and a valuable addition to the conversation.

A caution! I'm not saying the poem can mean anything you want it to mean. If you start arguing that "Blues" is about kangaroos, I'm going to be skeptical. Which brings us to the other location of meaning, the obvious one: the text. The text is not doing much if it remains filed away on a shelf—it needs your reading to activate meaning—but we need to attend very carefully to what's on the page. If you want to argue for the kangaroo interpretation, you'll have to show me where those kangaroos are. The best analytical discussions are creative, surprising, and intrepid, but they are also always grounded in evidence from the text. Otherwise you leave the poem behind.

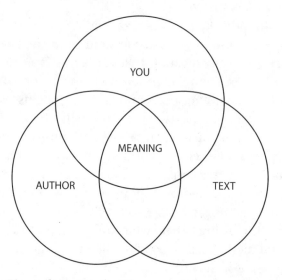

Above is the Venn diagram showing us where meaning is. You are always an important part of developing a poem's meaning. There it is, right out in the open, not hidden at all.

Poem Discussion One

Sonnet 130, by William Shakespeare

Sonnet 130

My mistress' eyes are nothing like the sun;
Coral is far more red than her lips' red;
If snow be white, why then her breasts are dun;°   *dull brown*
If hairs be wires, black wires grow on her head.
5 I have seen roses damasked,° red and white,   *mingled*
But no such roses see I in her cheeks,
And in some perfumes is there more delight
Than in the breath that from my mistress reeks.
I love to hear her speak, yet well I know
10 That music hath a far more pleasing sound;
I grant I never saw a goddess go —
My mistress, when she walks, treads on the ground.
    And yet, by heaven, I think my love as rare°   *extraordinary*
    As any she° belied° with false compare.   *woman, misrepresented*

                 —1609

WILLIAM SHAKESPEARE (1564–1616) WROTE this SONNET some time
in the 1590s, during the RENAISSANCE (also known as the Early Modern)
period. We might expect to find a poem written so long ago interest-
ing principally for what it shows us about its own cultural context.
What's remarkable here is that, from the first line, Shakespeare sub-
verts clichés that are still out in force in the love poetry of today. To
hear that the eyes of the SPEAKER's mistress "are nothing like the sun"
is still a pleasant surprise, deviating from the ubiquitous practice of
deploying SIMILES (her lips are like rubies, her eyes are like diamonds,
etc.), especially ones involving Nature, in the service of describing all
the features of a beloved.

We can trace these poetic commonplaces back to Francesco Petrarca (1304–74), in English referred to simply as Petrarch, an Italian poet sometimes nicknamed the "father of the Renaissance." His collection, the *Canzoniere*, included 317 sonnets in praise of a woman named Laura; these sonnets popularized the form and inspired a deluge of love poetry in the centuries following. The Petrarchan formula adopted by many Renaissance poets involved an ardent speaker expressing praise for his unattainable fair-haired mistress, and offering an enumeration of her physical attributes, a catalogue of features called a BLAZON.

Bringing the fourteen-line sonnet form to England were Sir Thomas Wyatt and the Earl of Surrey. A few innovations were made in the translation of the form from Italian to English. Wyatt introduced a RHYMING COUPLET at the end, and Surrey established a rhyme scheme that differed from the Italian version. Assigning letters to indicate rhyming lines, the Italian (or Petrarchan) sonnet is organized *abbaabba*, and then *cdecde* or *cdcdcd*. The first eight lines are referred to as the OCTAVE, and we call the final six lines the SESTET. The shift in the rhyme scheme between the two parts often reflects a shift in thought; there's commonly a turn, or VOLTA, at the beginning of the sestet, a move sometimes incorporated into the new English forms. The rhyme scheme Surrey developed proceeds as *ababcdcdefefgg*, an innovation born of necessity: English doesn't offer the wealth of similar endings we find in the Romance languages! The rhyme scheme sets a pattern of three QUATRAINS and one rhyming couplet, a kind of finale that can encapsulate the idea of the sonnet, offer a complicating layer, resolve tensions, or perform a kind of concluding volta. While these and other poets inaugurated the production of sonnets in England, the original genius of Shakespeare's work in this form explains why the other term for the English sonnet is the Shakespearean sonnet.

Another feature of this poem typical of Shakespearean sonnets lies in its METER, the rhythmic pattern of stressed and unstressed syllables. (For a concise introduction to metrical forms, see *A Brief Guide to Meter* [p. 111].) Here we see an example of IAMBIC PENTAMETER: the lines are made up of five two-syllable units, or feet, each FOOT comprised of an unstressed syllable followed by a stressed syllable. You can SCAN (determine the metrical pattern of) a line using the markings ´ (for accented syllables) and ˘ (for unaccented syllables):

˘ ⁄ ˘ ⁄ ˘ ⁄ ˘ ⁄ ˘ ⁄
My mistress' eyes are nothing like the sun;

That first line establishes clearly the iambic pentameter form. If you scan the entire poem, you will find that the majority of the lines follow this pattern precisely. But they don't all; look at line 2:

⁄ ˘ ˘ ⁄ ⁄ ⁄ ˘ ˘ ⁄ ⁄
Coral is far more red than her lips' red;

You will see these creative deviations from strict metrical patterns often in Shakespeare's works. While the deployment of iambic pentameter lends the sonnet an artful sense of music and literary gravity, the author's flexibility in its use precludes a sing-song monotony, offering instead the expressive modulations of a speaking voice. The resulting dynamic RHYTHM contributes to the forceful impact of the poem.

Many readers have viewed this poem as disparaging of its object. This mistress does not measure up to those ladies celebrated in the poems of Shakespeare's Elizabethan contemporaries. It might appear the speaker is frustrated at his love object's failure to measure up to the standards of beauty dictated by Petrarchan conventions. Shakespeare's use of "nothing" rather than "not" and "far more" rather than "more" imparts an emphatic tone to the speaker's

> **Research tip:** In many anthologies, you will see the word "reeks" glossed as 'exhales' or 'emanates,' the editors pointing out that usage in the Renaissance differed from current usage. Too bad, you might think, because reeking breath as we understand it would work so perfectly here! This is a case where you might want to do a little research yourself. The *Oxford English Dictionary*, which gives you the etymology (development and usage history) of words, indicates that both the noun and verb forms of "reek" had multiple meanings during the Renaissance, but the predominant usages relate to smoke (and some other meanings involve perspiration and bleeding). So negative connotation is possible. To pursue the question further you can consult a concordance. A concordance tracks

all the appearances of a particular word in the author's *oeuvre* (complete works). An online Shakespeare concordance (www. shakespeareswords.com) shows you every spot the word "reek" appears in the author's plays and poems. Reading through Shakespeare's various usages of "reek" suggests that, indeed, he often deployed the word in its more negative modes. In the play *Coriolanus*, for example, the incensed tragic hero shouts at the populace, "You common cry of curs! Whose breath I hate / As reek o'th' rotten fens" (Cor. III.iii.120–21). So while we've lost the more neutral sense of "reek," its negative connotations were available to, and adopted by, Shakespeare, and are likely in play in Sonnet 130.

observations. If other women's breasts are white as snow, his mistress has a dull brown bosom; if other women can boast hair as sparkling as the gold wire commonly adorning headdresses of the era, his mistress sports a darker metal. In every category of the conventional blazon, this mistress falls short.

The speaker proceeds to declare music more pleasant than his beloved's voice and confirms that her walk in no way resembles the movement of a goddess. Then we come upon the final rhyming couplet, and the argument turns. The major volta of the poem occurs here, signalled by the words "And yet," as the speaker proclaims that his mistress is just as admirable as women who are compared to coral and roses. It's interesting to see that there is a mild turn at the spot where the Petrarchan volta would traditionally appear, at the beginning of line 9. While for the first octave one could readily read the poem as entirely derogatory, line 9 begins, "I love to hear her speak," preparing the ground for the final couplet's celebration of an ordinary human woman.

The final two words of the poem are important ones: "false compare." Not only does the speaker's mistress not measure up to the claims of the traditional blazon, but other poets' love objects are equally misrepresented by them. So while this work has endured as a passionate defence of an unidealized woman, an unusual and striking love poem, its power lies also in its critique of the sonnet tradition. In other words, the poem is as much about poetry as it is about love.

Reading it through this lens, you can see that in every line the poet is revealing the absurdity of the blazon conventions widely practised by his fellow sonneteers. How could anybody's skin really be as white as snow? Do we seriously expect a mortal lover to prove herself a goddess? We can read the poem as a kind of anti-Petrarchan, or at least post-Petrarchan, sonnet.

This latter energy of the poem exemplifies the dynamic of INTERTEXTUALITY that enriches much of the literature you read. Intertextuality is the term we use to refer to all kinds of different relationships among texts. A poem might, for example, echo, allude to, even quote another poem. In the case of Sonnet 130, the intertextual relationship lies between a mass of Petrarchan poetry and Shakespeare's critique of that tradition. The conversations going on between texts, and between authors, will come into play as you, too, join the larger literary conversation.

More Sonnets by William Shakespeare

Note: Shakespeare wrote 154 sonnets, published together in 1609. While the final 28 (including Sonnet 130) are addressed to a figure known as the Dark Lady, the first 126 (including the following) are addressed to a young man.

Here are some questions to get you started:

Sonnet 18: How does this poem engage with Petrarchan conventions? *Sonnet 20*: How does gender complicate and enrich the tradition of the love sonnet here? (The historical and ongoing critical debate on homoeroticism/homosexuality in Shakespeare's sonnets is a fascinating avenue for research.) *Sonnet 73*: Why the uncertainty about the number of leaves in line 2? *Sonnet 116*: How does meaning shift if you deliver this poem in varying tones (earnest, sarcastic, cynical)?

Sonnet 18

Shall I compare thee to a summer's day?
Thou art more lovely and more temperate:
Rough winds do shake the darling buds of May,
And summer's lease hath all too short a date;
5 Sometime too hot the eye of heaven shines,
And often is his gold complexion dimmed;
And every fair° from fair sometime declines,   *beauty*
By chance or nature's changing course untrimmed: •
But thy eternal summer shall not fade,
10 Nor lose possession of that fair thou ow'st,°   *possess*
Nor shall Death brag thou wand'rest in his shade,
When in eternal lines to Time thou grow'st.
    So long as men can breathe, or eyes can see,
    So long lives this, and this gives life to thee.

—1609

Sonnet 20

A woman's face with Nature's own hand painted
Hast thou, the master-mistress of my passion;
A woman's gentle heart, but not acquainted
With shifting change, as is false women's fashion;
5 An eye more bright than theirs, less false in rolling,°   *straying*
Gilding the object whereupon it gazeth;
A man in hue,° all hues in his controlling,   *form*
Which steals men's eyes and women's souls amazeth.
And for° a woman wert thou first created,   *to be*
10 Till Nature as she wrought thee fell a-doting,
And by addition me of thee defeated,
By adding one thing to my purpose nothing.
    But since she pricked thee out for women's pleasure,
    Mine be thy love, and thy love's use their treasure.

—1609

Sonnet 73

That time of year thou mayst in me behold
When yellow leaves, or none, or few, do hang
Upon those boughs which shake against the cold,
Bare ruined choirs,¹ where late the sweet birds sang.
5 In me thou see'st the twilight of such day
As after sunset fadeth in the west,
Which by and by black night doth take away,
Death's second self, that seals up all in rest.
In me thou seest the glowing of such fire
10 That on the ashes of his youth doth lie,
As the death-bed whereon it must expire,
Consumed with that which it was nourished by.
    This thou perceiv'st, which makes thy love more strong,
    To love that well which thou must leave ere long.

—1609

Sonnet 116

Let me not to the marriage of true minds
Admit impediments; love is not love
Which alters when it alteration finds,
Or bends with the remover to remove.
5 O no, it is an ever-fixèd mark
That looks on tempests and is never shaken;
It is the star to every wand'ring bark,
Whose worth's unknown, although his height be taken.°   *measured*
Love's not Time's fool, though rosy lips and cheeks
10 Within his bending sickle's compass come:
Love alters not with his brief hours and weeks,
But bears it out even to the edge of doom.
    If this be error and upon me proved,
    I never writ, nor no man ever loved.

—1609

---

1 *choir*: area of church for choristers.

Poem Discussion Two
Harlem Dancer, by Claude McKay

Harlem Dancer

Applauding youths laughed with young prostitutes
And watched her perfect, half-clothed body sway;
Her voice was like the sound of blended flutes
Blown by black players upon a picnic day.
5 She sang and danced on gracefully and calm,
The light gauze hanging loose about her form;
To me she seemed a proudly-swaying palm
Grown lovelier for passing through a storm.
Upon her swarthy neck black, shiny curls
10 Profusely fell; and, tossing coins in praise,
The wine-flushed, bold-eyed boys, and even the girls,
Devoured her with their eager, passionate gaze:
But, looking at her falsely-smiling face,
I knew her self was not in that strange place.

—1922

HERE WE HAVE ANOTHER SONNET, this one written by Claude McKay (1889–1948). McKay was a leading poet of the HARLEM RENAISSANCE, a movement of the 1920s that saw a burst of creative activity among African Americans. McKay's collection *Harlem Shadows* (1922) was one of the books that launched the Harlem Renaissance.

Now that you are familiar with both Petrarchan conventions and the critique of those conventions in some of Shakespeare's sonnets, you are especially equipped to appreciate what McKay is doing here. We see the familiar focus on a female object, and a blazon is indicated by the words "body," "voice," "form," "neck," "curls" and "face." But this woman does not fulfil the virtuous ideal of the traditional sonnet;

this woman is dancing half-naked on a club stage, her challenging life experiences suggested figuratively by her "passing through a storm." Nor is this the golden-haired model of Petrarch and his followers. This woman has "swarthy" skin and "black" curls. The SIMILES McKay deploys underscore her racial difference from the expected object of sonnets. The instruments evoked by her voice are played by "black players," and her body is "a proudly-swaying palm," not a tree you'd find in Elizabethan England.

> **Research tip:** Nor, for that matter, would you find a palm in New York's Harlem neighbourhood. Here's a spot where some biographical research could prove useful. The palm tree points to a more Southern locale, and might pique your curiosity about McKay's history. A comprehensive resource for biographies is the *Dictionary of Literary Biography*, which is organized into hundreds of specialized volumes. Volume 45 covers *American Poets 1880–1945* and includes a biography of Claude McKay. You can also look up McKay in reference works such as *The Oxford Companion to Twentieth Century Poetry in English* or *The Encyclopedia of the Harlem Renaissance* (see Research Tip on p. 26 regarding encyclopedias). These sources reveal that McKay was born in Jamaica to peasant farmers, and moved to the United States in his early twenties. You might also look at some of McKay's other works, where you'll find a recurring nostalgia for rural Jamaica. Brief biographical sketches are readily available online, at open access sites such as *Poets.org*.

McKay contests a standard of beauty, governing RENAISSANCE love poetry (and still dominant today), that extols the white-skinned blonde. One of the things this sonnet does is celebrate the beauty of African American women, arguing that their features are equally worthy of praise. And the difficult life of this particular dancer, he stresses, has made her "lovelier" than a pampered, sheltered love object. Clearly she is enchanting, as evidenced by the "passionate gaze" of her audience.

But this is where McKay's second level of critique comes in. Note that "gaze" is joined in this short poem by the words "watched" and

"Kermis / The Peasant Dance" Pieter Bruegel the Elder, c. 1568.

"Spring Showers" Alfred Stieglitz, 1902.

"Sardines" Michael Goldberg, 1955.

"looking." The appearance of these synonymous terms points to look-ing as one of the themes of the work. The speaker's striking use of the word "Devoured" in line 12 conveys his judgement of the dynamic in play as the audience consumes the dance. Or, rather, the dancer. The audience is characterized as predatory, feeding on the appealing attributes detailed by our speaker. The final couplet shifts the focus, as the speaker notes the dancer's "falsely-smiling face." It's in her face that he can see a hint of *her* feelings, her own identity. He realizes that her "self was not in that strange place," her self separating off from the physical body which has been described in the poem. This observation throws into relief the objectifying thrust of the sonnet form. It's conventionally the body that is described, not the personal-ity. What's more, this poem puts us in mind of the lopsidedness of the traditional sonnet; while sonnets have purportedly been about desired women, they are really about the desirer, because his self is the only self we learn anything about. McKay's poem gestures toward the silenced subjectivity of the love object; notably, it can only be a gesture—the speaker can see the "self" is not there, but has no further access to it.

The Harlem Renaissance was more than an artistic movement. It was also a political project, as writers, artists and intellectuals in the African American community protested the racism of the era—epitomized by segregationist Jim Crow laws and continued lynchings—and promoted the creative accomplishments of blacks in America, both past and present. Many writers refused the forms dominating the cultural landscape and looked to their own heritage for inspiration. The poet Langston Hughes, for example, built upon Negro spirituals and the Blues, original African American genres. Why, then, would McKay choose to adopt the traditional European form of the sonnet?

One reason for writing sonnets was that they provided the perfect showcase, a way to display literary prowess in a form respected by the dominant culture. James Weldon Johnson, a leading intellectual of the Harlem Renaissance, claimed that "No people that has produced great literature and art has ever been looked upon by the world as distinctly inferior.... And nothing will do more to change that men-tal attitude and raise his status than a demonstration of intellectual parity by the Negro through the production of literature and art" (5). If social and political equality could arise from a recognition of artistic equality, how better to prove one's excellence to the establishment than to compose in the valued and enduring form of the sonnet?

McKay's stylistic choice might appear conservative, but in his introduction to *Harlem Shadows*, he makes clear his position on form:

> ... although very conscious of the new criticisms and trends in poetry, to which I am keenly responsive and receptive, I have adhered to such of the older traditions as I find adequate for my most lawless and revolutionary passions and moods.

For McKay, the centuries-old sonnet was the most revolutionary choice *because* it had been a vehicle through which Eurocentric values were promulgated. In other words, a form that produces in the reader a set of conventional expectations (for example, that a white woman's physical beauty will be described) is ripe for intervention. A value-laden form can be used in the service of a particularly forceful critique of those very values.

A poetic form with a long history is a kind of cultural repository. As soon as we encounter a fourteen-line poem, all manner of expectations (what the poem will be about, how the rhyme scheme will proceed, etc.) begin to build. McKay's work exemplifies the power of intervening in those expectations. Here we have another illustration of this book's principal lesson: form means. If bp Nichol's poem demonstrates how the spatial organization of letters and words can contribute to meaning, McKay's poem makes clear, in his revisioning of the sonnet, the meanings transmitted through traditional form.

More Poems by Writers of the Harlem Renaissance

Some questions to get you started:

"The Castaways": How does the initial octave mean differently after we read the final sestet? "Tableau": What is the effect of Cullen's chosen form here, the traditional English BALLAD? "The Weary Blues": How does Hughes set up the relationship between the speaker and the

Blues player? (Note, for example, the ambiguous referent of the "I" in line 3.) "Letter to My Sister": What does the PARADOX of "Breathless must your breath come through" reveal about life for African American women at this time?

The Castaways

The vivid grass with visible delight
Springing triumphant from the pregnant earth;
And butterflies, and sparrows in brief flight
Chirping and dancing for the season's birth,
5   And dandelions and rare daffodils
That hold the deep-stirred heart with hands of gold
And thrushes sending forth their joyous trills;
Not these, not these did I at first behold:
But seated on the benches daubed with green,
10 The castaways of earth, some fast asleep,
With many a withered woman wedged between,
And over all life's shadows dark and deep:
Moaning I turned away, for misery
I have the strength to bear but not to see.
                                   —Claude McKay, 1922

Tableau

Locked arm in arm they cross the way,
     The black boy and the white,
The golden splendor of the day,
     The sable pride of night.

5   From lowered blinds the dark folk stare,
     And here the fair folk talk,
Indignant that these two should dare
     In unison to walk.

Oblivious to look and word
10   They pass, and see no wonder

That lightning brilliant as a sword
    Should blaze the path of thunder.

                    —Countee Cullen, 1925

The Weary Blues

Droning a drowsy syncopated tune,
Rocking back and forth to a mellow croon,
    I heard a Negro play.
Down on Lenox Avenue° the other night   *main route through Harlem*
5 By the pale dull pallor of an old gas light
    He did a lazy sway ...
    He did a lazy sway ...
To the tune o' those Weary Blues.
With his ebony hands on each ivory key
10 He made that poor piano moan with melody.
    O Blues!
Swaying to and fro on his rickety stool
He played that sad raggy tune like a musical fool.
    Sweet Blues!
15 Coming from a black man's soul.
    O Blues!
In a deep song voice with a melancholy tone
I heard that Negro sing, that old piano moan—
    "Ain't got nobody in all this world,
20   Ain't got nobody but ma self.
    I's gwine to quit ma frownin'
    And put ma troubles on the shelf."
Thump, thump, thump, went his foot on the floor.
He played a few chords then he sang some more—
25   "I got the Weary Blues
    And I can't be satisfied.
    Got the Weary Blues
    And can't be satisfied—
    I ain't happy no mo'
30   And I wish that I had died."
And far into the night he crooned that tune.

The stars went out and so did the moon.
The singer stopped playing and went to bed
While the Weary Blues echoed through his head.
35 He slept like a rock or a man that's dead.

—Langston Hughes, 1925

Letter to My Sister

It is dangerous for a woman to defy the gods;
To taunt them with the tongue's thin tip,
Or strut in the weakness of mere humanity,
Or draw a line daring them to cross;
5   The gods own the searing lightning,
The drowning waters, tormenting fears
And anger of red sins.

Oh, but worse still if you mince timidly—
Dodge this way or that, or kneel or pray,
10 Be kind, or sweat agony drops
Or lay your quick body over your feeble young;
If you have beauty or none, if celibate
Or vowed—the gods are Juggernaut,[1]
Passing over ... over ...

15 This you may do:
Lock your heart, then, quietly,
And lest they peer within,
Light no lamp when dark comes down
Raise no shade for sun;
20 Breathless must your breath come through
If you'd die and dare deny
The gods their god-like fun.

—Anne Spencer, 1927

---

1   *Juggernaut*: Here a reference to huge temple wagons bearing statues of Hindu gods,
    rumoured to crush devotees under their wheels.

Poem Discussion Three

I, Being Born a Woman and Distressed, by Edna St. Vincent Millay

I, Being Born a Woman and Distressed

I, being born a woman and distressed
By all the needs and notions of my kind,
Am urged by your propinquity° to find   *nearness, proximity*
Your person fair, and feel a certain zest
5 To bear your body's weight upon my breast:
So subtly is the fume of life designed,
To clarify the pulse and cloud the mind,
And leave me once again undone, possessed.
Think not for this, however, the poor treason
10 Of my stout blood against my staggering brain,
I shall remember you with love, or season°   *temper, moderate*
My scorn with pity,—let me make it plain:
I find this frenzy insufficient reason
For conversation when we meet again.

—1923

LIKE CLAUDE MCKAY, EDNA St. Vincent Millay (1892–1950) chose the traditional form of the SONNET through which to challenge ideas associated with that genre. Here we get a woman's point of view, the conventional object of the sonnet talking back.

Line 2 introduces the vague phrase "needs and notions of my kind," raising the question of how an early twentieth-century reader would have interpreted that. What were the popularly conceived desires and dreams of a woman at that time? Women had just won the right to vote in the United States (in 1920) and were gaining some ground in the areas of paid work and higher education. Millay embodied the New Woman, that product of first-wave feminism who had untied her corsets, thought independently, and played a greater role in public life. Despite these advancements, however, social expectations for men and women still differed vastly. In romantic and sexual terms, the mainstream model for women of the early twentieth century resembled that of her nineteenth-century sisters. So the "needs and notions" of women would probably still translate to things like a romantic yet chaste courtship, monogamous marriage, and devotion to children.

> **Research tip:** To find out more about Edna St. Vincent Millay's cultural context, you can consult a subject encyclopedia. Subject encyclopedias (also called guides or companions) contain useful information, usually in the form of succinct, summarizing essays, relevant to a particular field, era, topic, etc. There's an *Encyclopedia of the Victorian Era*, for instance, and a *Companion to Renaissance Drama*. Print versions of these reference works usually appear as one hefty book, or a series of volumes. For your purposes here, you might look in a series such as *Feminism and Literature*. Volume 4 of that series covers twentieth-century topics, and within that volume you'll find a section entitled "Women in the Early to Mid-20th Century," and within that section you'll find a chapter called "Social and Economic Conditions." Finding the information you seek is just a matter of narrowing down your focus, a process facilitated by these user-friendly reference works.

Reading on, it becomes clear that what Millay means by "needs and notions" is sexual desire. Here we get woman as sexual subject rather than sexual object. While features of her body appear—"breast," "pulse," "blood," "brain"—they are far from decorative items in a blazon; they are the loci of feeling. At the end of the octave, the SPEAKER is "undone, possessed."

While the explicit sexual scenario is atypical for the sonnet (which conventionally figures unrequited love) those words would seem to place her in a stereotypically passive role.

But a closer reading reveals that the speaker is not exactly "possessed" by the lover. Rather she is overwhelmed by the "fume of life," "a certain zest": lust. It is her own desiring body, her biological drives, in other words, which can "cloud the mind" and overpower her. If McKay's dancer exhibited a split between her body ("Devoured" by her audience) and her mind ("not in that strange place"), Millay's speaker experiences the body/mind tension internally.

The particularity of this lover, then, is not very important. Note that word, "propinquity." I had to look it up when I first read this poem. Whenever you encounter an unusual new word, it pays to search for a definition; meanings often hinge on these oddball terms. As your gloss here indicates, propinquity means nearness, or proximity. So it's not that this person is beloved; they may not even be that charming or attractive. The lust here is merely a matter of pheromone exchange.

The rhyme scheme is that of the Italian sonnet, and a Petrarchan VOLTA does operate at line 9, flagged by the word "however." The final SESTET is resolutely anti-romantic, underscoring that while physical union may take place, the act does not indicate any serious interest on the part of the speaker. The two participants need not even speak again, the couplet declares.

It might be interesting to dig into Edna St. Vincent Millay's biography to learn more about her own romantic history. She and many of her contemporaries refused mainstream sexual mores. What's particularly powerful is how this poem speaks back, intertextually, to a CANON of love poetry that figured women as silent and asexual, chastely resistant to the passionate pleas of male speakers. In this 1923 poem, Millay dashes the long-held cultural binary (still at work today) that men are often "only after one thing" while women are apt to confuse sex with love. This sonnet takes up the issue of who defines our "needs and notions." As with "Harlem Dancer," such a challenge to cultural norms is all the more effective for being composed in the very form that has historically absorbed, conveyed and shaped those norms.

More Modern and Contemporary Sonnets

Consider the ways the following poems engage with the traditional form of the sonnet.

Poetics Against the Angel of Death

I am sorry to speak of death again
(some say I'll have a long life)
but last night Wordsworth's 'Prelude'
suddenly made sense—I mean the measure,
5   the elevated tone, the attitude
of private Man speaking to public men.
Last night I thought I would not wake again
but now with this June morning I run ragged to elude
The Great Iambic Pentameter
10   who is the Hound of Heaven[1] in our stress
because I want to die
writing Haiku
or, better,
long lines, clean and syllabic as knotted bamboo. Yes!
                              —Phyllis Webb, 1962

Nothing in That Drawer

Nothing in that drawer.
Nothing in that drawer.
Nothing in that drawer.
Nothing in that drawer.
5   Nothing in that drawer.
Nothing in that drawer.
Nothing in that drawer.
Nothing in that drawer.

---

1   *Hound of Heaven*: ALLUSION to poem by Francis Thomson, in which God is figured as ever in pursuit of the wayward speaker.

Nothing in that drawer.
10 Nothing in that drawer.
Nothing in that drawer.
Nothing in that drawer.
Nothing in that drawer.
Nothing in that drawer.

—Ron Padgett, 1969

Sonnet #15

Time of, dress warmly, 3 AM walk
Coat over sweater, shawl over
Hair, boots over slippers, snow
On & over all, I forgot
5 To mention I'm drunk (martini
& piece of toast) I think
Our traffic signal's remarkable
In the air, 2 wires & 2 streets
Cross exactly there. I cross
10 On green, the snow, making tracks
To a white beach, a long time's
Sliding into bed, reaching
To feel you, in place, in place I
With snow, on my hair, on the sheet

—Alice Notley, 1971

so'net 1

```
so no n so no n so no toes
toe no n toe no n toe so nose
so no n toe no n so toe nose
t toe no nose no toe so nose
5  toe t nose t toe nose toes
so nose t toes n nose nose toes
o nose o nose o nose n toes
o o o no o so toe nose
```

```
    nose s toes n toes s nose
10  so toes n nose no t so nose toe
    t nose no toe s t not no nose
    n so not t nose s t no not toe
      no toe nose not t no no nose
       n no nose nose not t no no toes
```

—Paul Dutton, 1979

Sonnet for Bonnie

—Darren Wershler-Henry, 1997

Dim Lady

My honeybunch's peepers are nothing like neon. Today's special at Red Lobster is redder than her kisser. If Liquid Paper is white, her racks are institutional beige. If her mop were Slinkys, dishwater Slinkys would grow on her noggin. I have seen table-
5   cloths in Shakey's Pizza Parlors, red and white, but no such picnic colors do I see in her mug. And in some minty-fresh mouthwashes there is more sweetness than in the garlic breeze my main squeeze wheezes. I love to hear her rap, yet I'm aware that

Muzak has a hipper beat. I don't know any Marilyn Monroes.
10 My ball and chain is plain from head to toe. And yet, by gosh,
my scrumptious twinkie has as much sex appeal for me as any
lanky model or platinum movie idol who's hyped beyond belief.

                              —Harryette Mullen, 2002

Poem Discussion Four

The Dance, by William Carlos Williams

The Dance

In Brueghel's great picture, The Kermess,
the dancers go round, they go round and
around, the squeal and the blare and the
tweedle of bagpipes, a bugle and fiddles
5 tipping their bellies (round as the thick-
sided glasses whose wash they impound)
their hips and their bellies off balance
to turn them. Kicking and rolling
about the Fair Grounds, swinging their butts, those
10 shanks must be sound to bear up under such
rollicking measures, prance as they dance
in Brueghel's great picture, The Kermess.

—1944

[See "Kermis / The Peasant Dance" in the colour insert.]

THE FIRST LINE OF William Carlos Williams's (1883–1963) "The Dance" announces itself as an EKPHRASTIC POEM, a poem which responds to a work of visual art. The SPEAKER proceeds to describe Bruegel's scene of peasants enjoying a village fair. Reading the poem (especially aloud), however, one starts to feel this is more than a description; somehow Williams manages to *embody* the energy of a painting which itself manages to embody the movement and clamour of a peasant festival. How does he do it?

The first thing you probably notice is the RHYTHM of this poem, which is rollicking and wild. If you SCAN the lines, you'll find the dominant pattern is of a stressed syllable followed by two unstressed syllables (´ ˘ ˘). This is **DACTYLIC METER**, familiar to us in various dance genres, such as waltzes. But the meter is not regular in the poem; an extra stress here, a dropped unstress there—these hiccups in the rhythmic flow refuse a steady beat. Another way we are kept off balance is through the distribution of the metric feet across the lines. In Shakespeare's sonnets we saw five **IAMBIC FEET** organized tidily within each line. Here the feet run over the end of one line and into the next, so that some lines have three stresses, some four. Line nine features five stressed syllables. The infectious dactylic meter, punctuated by blurts and skips, produces a rhythm highly evocative of the inebriated dancing depicted in the painting.

Not only the rhythm, but the **SYNTAX** spills over line endings in Williams's poem. The entire poem is comprised of only two sentences, so that sense is necessarily carried along from line to line. More noticeable, however, are the line endings featuring clearly incomplete thoughts and phrases. Endings such as "and," "the," "thick-," "those" and "such" pre-empt the habitual pause readers take upon the completion of a line and compel us to swing over into the next line. This technique is called **ENJAMBMENT**. The literal (French) meaning of the term, "a straddling"—picture one leg planted at the end of one line, the other stretching down into the next—seems particularly relevant to this corporeal poem. We "go round and / around." The only full stop is a **CAESURA**, appearing in the middle of line eight when the poem is at full momentum and catching us off guard. In line seven we are told the dancers are "off balance," an assessment dramatically conveyed through Williams's effective choreography of syntactical and stress patterns.

Other details of the poem further evoke the dizzying energy of the scene. Note the parenthetical phrase describing bellies: "(round as the thick- / sided glasses whose wash they impound.)" The **SIMILE** comparing bellies to glasses alerts us to other spots in the poem where there's an overlap or blurring of terms. Consider the phrase "the squeal and the blare and the / tweedle of bagpipes, a bugle and fiddles." Three sounds for three instruments: bagpipes squeal, the bugle blares and fiddles tweedle. But the lineation and punctuation allow for the **ONOMATOPOEIA** "tweedle" to be paired with bagpipes. So maybe bagpipes tweedle, the bugle blares and fiddles squeal. The onomatopoeiac words make for a noisy poem, but the commotion is made all the more lively and vertiginous by the syntactical ambiguity. To compound the ambiguity, the phrase that follows is "tipping their bellies," in which "their" seems momentarily to refer to the instruments before we recall the dancers who were introduced as the principal subject of the poem. If you read through the first sentence, the last word, "them," could conceivably refer to a) the dancers, b) the glasses, and/or c) the instruments. The dancers are "swinging their butts," moving their behinds, but a "butt" is also a cask for alcohol and a "sackbutt" is a medieval form of trombone. It's no accident Williams chose the word "sound" rather than 'sturdy' or 'strong' to characterize the dancers' legs. The poet has composed this poem so that there are numerous instances of blur among the people, glasses, and instruments in the scene. These overlaps are apt, because all three terms are vessels of celebration, but more importantly they contribute to the kinetic, joyful, off-balance embodiment that is this poem.

You probably noticed that the last line of "The Dance" echoes the first. When you notice something like that, the important next step is to ask yourself, "Why? How does this compositional feature contribute to the effect of the poem?" A couple of things come to mind here. We know the dancers "go round and / around"; to repeat the first line is to bring us full circle ourselves and perhaps to suggest an ongoing loop as the festival continues. The repeated line also forms a kind of frame, evoking the painting at the heart of Williams's vision here. To my mind this frame only emphasizes all the excess and spilling and blurring explicated above; this is a poem that will not be contained. Now look at Bruegel's work. Does his festival scene fall neatly within the borders of the painting?

More Ekphrastic Poems

Some questions to get you started:

"Young Sycamore": Critic Bram Dijkstra has proposed that Williams's poem was written in response to this Stieglitz photograph. In what ways does reading the poem mirror viewing the photograph, and echo also the growth of the tree? "Venus Transiens": Venus Transiens, or the Transit of Venus, is an astronomical event during which Venus comes between Earth and the sun; how does this title contribute to the meaning of the poem? "Preciosilla": Stein's piece responds not to a static visual art work, but rather to the music and dance of Spanish flamenco; listen for the dramatic rhythms, but consider also the meanings of the words, not chosen for sound alone. View online videos of flamenco for reference. "Why I Am Not a Painter": How does the poem explore the differences and similarities between visual art and writing? "from *Pictograms from the Interior of B.C.*": Fred Wah calls his poetic responses to John Corner's reproductions of aboriginal rock paintings "transcreations" (Interview 34). How does this term help characterize his particular ekphrastic process here?

[See "Spring Showers" in the colour insert.]

Young Sycamore

I must tell you
this young tree
whose round and firm trunk
between the wet

5　pavement and the gutter
(where water
is trickling) rises
bodily

into the air with
10　one undulant
thrust half its height—
and then

dividing and waning
sending out
15　young branches on
all sides—

hung with cocoons—
it thins
till nothing is left of it
20　but two

eccentric knotted
twigs
bending forward
hornlike at the top

—William Carlos Williams, 1927

[See "The Birth of Venus" in the colour insert.]

Venus Transiens

Tell me,
Was Venus more beautiful
Than you are,
When she topped
5   The crinkled waves,
Drifting shoreward
On her plaited shell?
Was Botticelli's vision
Fairer than mine;
10 And were the painted rosebuds
He tossed his lady
Of better worth
Than the words I blow about you
To cover your too great loveliness
15 As with a gauze
Of misted silver?

For me,
You stand poised
In the blue and buoyant air,
20 Cinctured by bright winds,
Treading the sunlight.
And the waves which precede you
Ripple and stir
The sands at my feet.

—Amy Lowell, 1915

Manuela Vargas at a dress rehearsal for "The Tigress of the Flamenco,"
1964. Dennis Oulds / Hulton Archive / Copyright © Getty Images.

Preciosilla

Cousin to Clare washing.

In the win all the band beagles which have cousin lime sign and ar-
range a weeding match to presume a certain point to exstate to exstate
a certain pass lint to exstate a lean sap prime lo and shut shut is life.

5   Bait, bait, tore, tore her clothes, toward it, toward a bit, to ward a sit,
sit down in, in vacant surely lots, a single mingle, bait and wet, wet a
single establishment that has a lily lily grow. Come to the pen come in
the stem, come in the grass grown water.

Lily wet lily wet while. This is so pink so pink in stammer, a long
10 bean which shows bows is collected by a single curly shady, shady get,
get set wet bet.

It is a snuff a snuff to be told and have can wither, can is it and sleep
sleeps knot, it is a lily scarf the pink and blue yellow, not blue not odour
sun, nobles are bleeding bleeding two seats two seats on end. Why is
15 grief. Grief is strange black. Sugar is melting. We will not swim.

Preciosilla

Please be please be get, please get wet, wet naturally, naturally in
weather. Could it be fire more firier. Could it be so in ate struck. Could
it be gold up, gold up stringing, in it while while which is hanging,
20 hanging in dingling, dingling in pinning, not so. Not so dots large
dressed dots, big sizes, less laced, less laced diamonds, diamonds
white, diamonds bright, diamonds in the in the light, diamonds light
diamonds door diamonds hanging to be four, two four, all before, this
bean, lessly, all most, a best, willow, vest, a green guest, guest, go go go
25 go go go, go. Go go. Not guessed. Go go.

Toasted susie is my ice-cream.

—Gertrude Stein, 1926

[See "Sardines" in the colour insert.]

Why I Am Not a Painter

I am not a painter, I am a poet.
Why? I think I would rather be
a painter, but I am not. Well,

for instance, Mike Goldberg
5 is starting a painting. I drop in.
"Sit down and have a drink" he
says. I drink; we drink. I look
up. "You have SARDINES in it."
"Yes, it needed something there."
10 "Oh." I go and the days go by
and I drop in again. The painting
is going on, and I go, and the days
go by. I drop in. The painting is
finished. "Where's SARDINES?"
15 All that's left is just
letters, "It was too much," Mike says.

But me? One day I am thinking of
a color: orange. I write a line
about orange. Pretty soon it is a
20 whole page of words, not lines.
Then another page. There should be
so much more, not of orange, of
words, of how terrible orange is
and life. Days go by. It is even in
25 prose, I am a real poet. My poem
is finished and I haven't mentioned
orange yet. It's twelve poems, I call
it ORANGES. And one day in a gallery
I see Mike's painting, called SARDINES.

—Frank O'Hara, 1957

from **Pictograms from the Interior of B.C.**

nv s ble

tr ck

—Fred Wah, 1975

Poem Discussion Five
Ode on a Grecian Urn, by John Keats

Ode on a Grecian Urn

I

Thou still unravish'd bride of quietness,
    Thou foster-child of silence and slow time,
Sylvan° historian, who canst thus express   *of the woods*
    A flowery tale more sweetly than our rhyme:
5 What leaf-fring'd legend haunts about thy shape
    Of deities or mortals, or of both,
        In Tempe or the dales of Arcady?[1]
What men or gods are these? What maidens loth?
    What mad pursuit? What struggle to escape?
10   What pipes and timbrels? What wild ecstasy?

2

Heard melodies are sweet, but those unheard
    Are sweeter; therefore, ye soft pipes, play on;
Not to the sensual ear, but, more endear'd,°   *valuable, cherished*
    Pipe to the spirit ditties of no tone:
15 Fair youth, beneath the trees, thou canst not leave
    Thy song, nor ever can those trees be bare;
        Bold Lover, never, never canst thou kiss,
Though winning near the goal—yet, do not grieve;
    She cannot fade, though thou hast not thy bliss,
20   Forever wilt thou love, and she be fair!

---

1 *Tempe, Arcady*: Beautiful, rustic regions of ancient Greece.

3

Ah, happy, happy boughs! that cannot shed
   Your leaves, nor ever bid the Spring adieu;
And, happy melodist, unwearied,
   For ever piping songs for ever new;
25 More happy love! more happy, happy love!
    For ever warm and still to be enjoy'd,
     Forever panting, and forever young;
All breathing human passion far above,
   That leaves a heart high-sorrowful and cloy'd,
30   A burning forehead, and a parching tongue.

4

Who are these coming to the sacrifice?
   To what green altar, O mysterious priest,
Lead'st thou that heifer lowing at the skies,
   And all her silken flanks with garlands dressed?
35 What little town by river or sea shore,
   Or mountain-built with peaceful citadel,°   *fortress*
    Is emptied of this folk, this pious morn?
And, little town, thy streets for evermore
   Will silent be, and not a soul to tell
40   Why thou art desolate, can e'er return.

5

O Attic[1] shape! Fair attitude! with brede°   *pattern, braid*
   Of marble men and maidens overwrought,
With forest branches and the trodden weed;
   Thou, silent form, dost tease us out of thought
45 As doth eternity: Cold Pastoral!
    When old age shall this generation waste,
     Thou shalt remain, in midst of other woe

---

1 *Attic*: From Attica, site of Athens.

Than ours, a friend to man, to whom thou say'st,
  "Beauty is truth, truth beauty,"—that is all
50   Ye know on earth, and all ye need to know.

—1820

HERE WE HAVE ANOTHER EKPHRASTIC POEM, written by the ROMANTIC poet, John Keats (1795–1821). The urn in the poem did not actually exist, but rather is an imaginary composite based on the designs of various ancient urns Keats had studied. The poem is an ODE, featuring the urn as an object inspiring admiration, awe, and meditation. The speaker addresses the urn directly, a rhetorical device termed an APOSTROPHE.

One of the first things you might notice is that there are a lot of question marks in this poem, especially in the initial STANZA. These question marks convey the disposition of the SPEAKER: curious, engaged, stimulated. He is fascinated by this ancient artifact that can "express / A flowery tale more sweetly than our rhyme," bespeaking a writer's envy of visual art. More particularly, he is enthralled by the longevity of this artifact, and enters into the world of the scenes depicted on the urn as a way to explore the rift between those permanent, immortal images and his own mortal existence.

PARADOXES abound in the poem. At the end of the first stanza we read about scenes of "mad pursuit" and "wild ecstasy," yet these highly dynamic dramas are portrayed through a still image. How can it be that "Heard melodies are sweet, but those unheard / Are sweeter"? Is it because reality can never measure up to the imagination, a force the Romantics were very interested in? Is it because a heard melody exists in time, having a duration and therefore an end, whereas an unheard melody might exceed time? The paradox of the "Bold Lover" captivates the speaker; while the forever unrequited love might seem an agony, the speaker exclaims that this guarantees the permanence of desire, youth, and beauty.

The exclamations rise to a pitch in the third stanza, always involving the word "happy," which appears six times. What is the effect of this repetition? Does it convey the intensity of the speaker's envy? Is it so excessive that it betrays the opposite to you, a faltering conviction that immortality is a desirable state? Might it even suggest a loss for words, the speaker repeating himself the way a person does when emotion takes over? Do you notice that I am asking a lot of questions?

The speaker's questions return in stanza four as he meditates upon another depiction on the urn, that of the procession. The scene includes a priest, a sacrificial animal, and a group of villagers. What's especially interesting here is that the speaker begins asking questions about what is *not* in the scene. When he asks "To what green altar" the priest leads the crowd, we can imagine him turning the urn in his hands to see if it depicts where they are going. When he asks "What little town" they come from, we can imagine him turning the urn the other way. That he wonders if the town is "by river or sea shore, / Or mountain-built" signals that the town is not depicted on the urn, but is instead the product of speculation, imagination. How striking it is, then, when he goes on to address this imaginary town at the end of the stanza. The tone becomes mournful at this point, but why? Does the permanent desolation of a town vacated of its inhabitants evidence the speaker's disillusionment with the eternal yet fixed world of the urn? Does the angst centre around the phrase, "not a soul to tell," the absence of answers to all the speaker's questions?

After investigating the scenes on the urn, the speaker concludes with a passionate apostrophe to the urn itself, encapsulating its paradoxical nature in the OXYMORONIC term, "Cold Pastoral!" In literature, PASTORAL scenes celebrate an idyllic existence in the verdant countryside, yet here the images of rustic vitality are frozen. The speaker's fascination with the immortality of art is plainly stated in the lines, "When old age shall this generation waste, / Thou shalt remain, in midst of other woe." These qualities of the urn are what "tease us out of thought," an odd phrase, it might seem, because the urn has teased the speaker *into* thought, into meditation. But this thinking is perhaps of a kind that exceeds pragmatic thought, escapes reason. The paradoxical power of this object has launched the speaker into an exceptional contemplative state, one propelled by multiple questions and then, in the final stanza, culminating in a summative, but extremely enigmatic statement, "Beauty is truth, truth beauty." This doubled equation of loaded abstractions spurs the reader's own meditative powers; its meaning cannot be digested readily. Instead, the

Research tip: The enigmatic conclusion of "Ode on a Grecian Urn" has inspired much critical discussion. It's fascinating to track the history of responses to this poem, and all the back-and-forth critical arguments addressing, particularly, its concluding lines. An excellent database of critical articles is the *MLA International Bibliography*, which most libraries subscribe to. If you type the poem's title into the *MLA International Bibliography* search box, you'll see hundreds of articles published in literary journals dating back to 1925. Reading these articles you'll discover, for example, the controversy over who is addressing whom at the very end of the poem. Is this urn continuing to address humanity? Is the speaker addressing the reader? The urn? The compelling mystery of the poem's conclusion has kept the discussion alive. If you read across the decades, you'll probably notice that while the mid-twentieth-century critics aim to argue a case, to prove a particular reading, later critics reveal more comfort with multiple possibilities, with INDETERMINACY. This difference marks the shift in approach from the earlier school of NEW CRITICISM, to later theoretical approaches such as DECONSTRUCTION, READER-RESPONSE CRITICISM, and NEW HISTORICISM. Contemporary critical treatments tend to be more accepting of uncertainty; perhaps we are acquiring a kind of negative capability! Exciting new readings keep appearing; see, for instance, Thomas Dilworth's article "Beauty and Truth: The Shakespearean Proto-text for Keats's 'Grecian Urn'" (2015), in which he identifies a probable INTERTEXT for the poem in Shakespeare's "The Phoenix and the Turtle," which contains the lines, "Truth and Beauty buried be. // To this urn let those repair...."

puzzling phrase invites us into a state akin to the speaker's. This might remind you of the process inspired by zen koans, paradoxical questions that prompt meditation and ultimately an awareness outside the realm of reason. (A well-known example of a koan: What is the sound of one hand clapping?) Keats was very interested in contemplative states that pushed one beyond our habitual drive for mastery and intellectual comprehension. In a letter to his brothers, he describes something he calls NEGATIVE CAPABILITY, a state in which someone is "capable of being in uncertainties, mysteries, doubts, without any irritable reaching after fact and reason" (*Letters* 48).

One of the things I love about this poem is the chiastic structure of its signature phrase. A CHIASMUS is a literary figure in which the second half repeats the first, in reverse order. To remember the pattern, just think of the Swedish pop group ABBA:

A   B   B   A
Beauty is truth, truth beauty

While the chiastic structure contributes to the enigmatic quality of this famous phrase, it also chimes perfectly with the action of the poem. Recall the speaker turning the urn this way and that in his hands. When you rotate a circular object, you look at this design then that, that design then this. ABBA. This energizing circuit between form and content contributes to the impact of this famous poem.

Like the urn in the speaker's hands, and like the chiasmus, the poem comes round, and comes round again in the minds of its readers, in the discussions of its critics. The curious, questioning attitude of the speaker toward the urn is one we readers adopt toward the poem itself (and would do well to cultivate in all our encounters with poetry). The critical conversation continues to evolve after a couple of centuries, leaving the door open for you to join in.

More Odes, Apostrophes, Addresses

Some questions to get you started:

"Ode to a Nightingale": Think about the connections and tensions between this Keatsian ode and his "Ode on a Grecian Urn" (consider, for example, his treatments of immortality and the imagination). "A Supermarket in California": How does the prose poetry form of this work contribute to its meaning? "July Man": How does setting figure into Avison's portrait of the man? "To My Twenties": In Kenneth Koch's book *New Addresses*, he apostrophizes some odd things (e.g. "To Piano Lessons," "To Marijuana," "To Duration"); what poetic

possibilities are opened up through this strategy? "Late One Night":
What new modes of address arise out of social media? How might
they yield new poetic forms?

Ode to a Nightingale

I

My heart aches, and a drowsy numbness pains
   My sense, as though of hemlock[1] I had drunk,
Or emptied some dull opiate to the drains
   One minute past, and Lethe-wards[2] had sunk:
5 'Tis not through envy of thy happy lot,
   But being too happy in thine happiness,—
      That thou, light-winged Dryad[3] of the trees,
      In some melodious plot
Of beechen° green, and shadows numberless,   *of the beech tree*
10   Singest of summer in full-throated ease.

2

O, for a draught of vintage! that hath been
   Cool'd a long age in the deep-delved earth,
Tasting of Flora° and the country green,   *Roman goddess of flowers*
   Dance, and Provençal[4] song, and sunburnt mirth!
15 O for a beaker full of the warm South,
   Full of the true, the blushful Hippocrene,[5]
      With beaded bubbles winking at the brim,
      And purple-stained mouth;
That I might drink, and leave the world unseen,
20   And with thee fade away into the forest dim:

---

1 *hemlock*: Poison made from hemlock plant.
2 *Lethe*: In Greek mythology, a river in the underworld which brought forgetfulness.
3 *Dryad*: In Greek mythology, a wood nymph.
4 *Provençal*: Of Provence, area of southern France associated with troubadours.
5 *Hippocrene*: In Greek mythology, a sacred fountain bringing poetic inspiration.

3

Fade far away, dissolve, and quite forget
    What thou among the leaves hast never known,
The weariness, the fever, and the fret
    Here, where men sit and hear each other groan;
25 Where palsy shakes a few, sad, last gray hairs,
      Where youth grows pale, and spectre-thin, and dies;
        Where but to think is to be full of sorrow
          And leaden-eyed despairs,
    Where Beauty cannot keep her lustrous eyes,
30   Or new Love pine at them beyond to-morrow.

4

Away! away! for I will fly to thee,
    Not charioted by Bacchus[1] and his pards,°   *leopards*
But on the viewless° wings of Poesy,   *invisible*
    Though the dull brain perplexes and retards:
35 Already with thee! tender is the night,
    And haply the Queen-Moon is on her throne,
      Cluster'd around by all her starry Fays;°   *fairies*
        But here there is no light,
    Save what from heaven is with the breezes blown
40   Through verdurous[2] glooms and winding mossy ways.

5

I cannot see what flowers are at my feet,
    Nor what soft incense hangs upon the boughs,
But, in embalmed° darkness, guess each sweet   *perfumed*
    Wherewith the seasonable month endows
45 The grass, the thicket, and the fruit-tree wild;
    White hawthorn, and the pastoral eglantine;°   *sweet briar, wild rose*
      Fast fading violets cover'd up in leaves;

---

1 *Bacchus*: Roman god of wine.
2 *verdurous*: lush with greenery.

And mid-May's eldest child,
The coming musk-rose, full of dewy wine,
50   The murmurous haunt of flies on summer eves.

6

Darkling° I listen; and, for many a time   *in the dark*
    I have been half in love with easeful Death,
Call'd him soft names in many a mused rhyme,
    To take into the air my quiet breath;
55 Now more than ever seems it rich to die,
    To cease upon the midnight with no pain,
        While thou art pouring forth thy soul abroad
            In such an ecstasy!
    Still wouldst thou sing, and I have ears in vain—
60   To thy high requiem° become a sod.   *musical composition for the dead*

7

Thou wast not born for death, immortal Bird!
    No hungry generations tread thee down;
The voice I hear this passing night was heard
    In ancient days by emperor and clown:
65 Perhaps the self-same song that found a path
    Through the sad heart of Ruth, when, sick for home,
        She stood in tears amid the alien corn;[1]
            The same that oft-times hath
    Charm'd magic casements, opening on the foam
70   Of perilous seas, in faery lands forlorn.

8

Forlorn! the very word is like a bell
    To toll me back from thee to my sole self!
Adieu! the fancy cannot cheat so well

---

1   *Ruth ... corn*: In the Biblical story, Ruth works as a gleaner, away from her native land.

As she is fam'd to do, deceiving elf.
75 Adieu! adieu! thy plaintive anthem fades
    Past the near meadows, over the still stream,
        Up the hill-side; and now 'tis buried deep
          In the next valley-glades:
    Was it a vision, or a waking dream?
80   Fled is that music:—Do I wake or sleep?

                       —John Keats, 1820

A Supermarket in California

What thoughts I have of you tonight, Walt Whitman, for
I walked down the sidestreets under the trees with a headache
self-conscious looking at the full moon.
    In my hungry fatigue, and shopping for images, I went
5 into the neon fruit supermarket, dreaming of your enumerations!
    What peaches and what penumbras![1] Whole families
shopping at night! Aisles full of husbands! Wives in the
avocados, babies in the tomatoes!—and you, Garcia Lorca, what
were you doing down by the watermelons?

10   I saw you, Walt Whitman, childless, lonely old grubber,
poking among the meats in the refrigerator and eyeing the grocery
boys.
    I heard you asking questions of each: Who killed the
pork chops? What price bananas? Are you my Angel?
15   I wandered in and out of the brilliant stacks of cans
following you, and followed in my imagination by the store
detective.
    We strode down the open corridors together in our
solitary fancy tasting artichokes, possessing every frozen
20 delicacy, and never passing the cashier.

    Where are we going, Walt Whitman? The doors close in
an hour. Which way does your beard point tonight?

---

1 *penumbras*: partial shadows.

(I touch your book and dream of our odyssey in the
supermarket and feel absurd.)
25   Will we walk all night through solitary streets? The
trees add shade to shade, lights out in the houses, we'll both be
lonely.

Will we stroll dreaming of the lost America of love
past blue automobiles in driveways, home to our silent cottage?
30   Ah, dear father, graybeard, lonely old courage-teacher,
what America did you have when Charon[1] quit poling his ferry and
you got out on a smoking bank and stood watching the boat
disappear on the black waters of Lethe?[2]

                              —Allen Ginsberg, 1956

July Man

Old, rain-wrinkled, time-soiled, city-wise, morning man
whose weeping is for the dust of the elm-flowers
and the hurting motes of time,
rotted with rotting grape,
5 sweet with the fumes,
puzzled for good by fermented potato-
peel out of the vat of the times,
turned out and left
in this grass-patch, this city-gardener's place
10 under the buzzing populace's
square shadows, and the green shadows
of elm and ginkgo and lime
(planted for Sunday strollers and summer evening
families, and for those
15 bird-cranks with bread-crumbs
and crumpled umbrellas who come
while the dew is wet on the park, and beauty
is fan-tailed, grey and dove grey, aslant, folding in
from the white fury of day).

---

1 *Charon*: In Greek mythology, ferryman of the newly dead.
2 *Lethe*: See p. 49, note 2.

20 In the sound of the fountain
    you rest, at the cinder-rim, on your bench.

    The rushing river of cars
    makes you a stillness, a pivot, a heart-stopping
    blurt, in the sorrow
25 of the last rubbydub swig, the searing, and
    stone-jar solitude lost, and yet,
    and still — wonder (for good now) and
    trembling:

        The too much none of us knows
30   is weight, sudden sunlight, falling
        on your hands and arms, in your lap,
        all, all, in time.

                              —Margaret Avison, 1966

To My Twenties

    How lucky that I ran into you
    When everything was possible
    For my legs and arms, and with hope in my heart
    And so happy to see any woman—
5   O woman! O my twentieth year!
    Basking in you, you
    Oasis from both growing and decay
    Fantastic unheard of nine- or ten-year oasis
    A palm tree, hey! And then another
10 And another—and water!
    I'm still very impressed by you. Whither,
    Midst falling decades, have you gone? Oh in what lucky fellow,
    Unsure of himself, upset, and unemployable
    For the moment in any case, do you live now?
15 From my window I drop a nickel
    By mistake. With
    You I race down to get it
    But I find there on

The street instead, a good friend,
20 X---- N----, who says to me
Kenneth do you have a minute?
And I say yes! I am in my twenties!
I have plenty of time! In you I marry,
In you I first go to France; I make my best friends
25 In you, and a few enemies. I
Write a lot and am living all the time
And thinking about living. I loved to frequent you
After my teens and before my thirties.
You three together in a bar
30 I always preferred you because you were midmost
Most lustrous apparently strongest
Although now that I look back on you
What part have you played?
You never, ever, were stingy. What you gave me you gave whole
35 But as for telling
Me how to best use it
You weren't a genius at that.
Twenties, my soul
Is yours for the asking
40 You know that, if you ever come back.

                              —Kenneth Koch, 2000

Late One Night

y wd I nd   wd I nd 2   i nd 2 spk   nd 2 spk 2
2 spk 2 u?   spk 2 u? y   2 u? y wd   u? y wd i

                              —Margaret Christakos, 2013

Poem Discussion Six

The Tyger, by William Blake

The Tyger

Tyger! Tyger! burning bright
In the forests of the night,
What immortal hand or eye
Could frame thy fearful symmetry?

5 In what distant deeps or skies
Burnt the fire of thine eyes?
On what wings dare he aspire?
What the hand dare seize the fire?

And what shoulder, & what art,
10 Could twist the sinews of thy heart?
And when thy heart began to beat,
What dread hand? & what dread feet?

What the hammer? what the chain,
In what furnace was thy brain?
15 What the anvil? what dread grasp
Dare its deadly terrors clasp?

When the stars threw down their spears
And water'd heaven with their tears,
Did he smile his work to see?
20 Did he who made the Lamb make thee?

Tyger! Tyger! burning bright
In the forests of the night,

What immortal hand or eye
Dare frame thy fearful symmetry?

—1794

LIKE KEATS'S "ODE ON a Grecian Urn," Blake's (1757–1827) "The Tyger" has long kept readers intrigued, inspiring much critical discussion. Another feature the two poems share is a SPEAKER with lots of questions. All the queries here point to the essential question of the poem: who could have created such a formidable beast?

Blake published "The Tyger" in *Songs of Experience*. Its companion poem, "The Lamb" (see below), appears in the companion volume *Songs of Innocence*. The question in line 20, "Did he who made the Lamb make thee?", invokes the Christian God, who sent Jesus Christ (traditionally referred to as the Lamb of God) to Earth. If the implied answer to the speaker's questions is God, the poem is addressing a puzzle familiar to people of faith: how could a divine creator allow "deadly terrors"—peril, catastrophes, pain, even evil—to exist?

There is a compelling physicality to the IMAGERY in the poem. Not only do we hear of the "eyes," "sinews," "heart," and "brain" of the tiger; we are also invited to consider the "hand," "eye," "wings," "shoulder," and "feet" of the maker. If the Christian Lamb is conventionally viewed as God incarnate (a physical manifestation of God), then how might this "fearful" creature embody its maker? Do the "burning," "fire," and "furnace" suggest another possible creator, one from the "deeps"?

The fourth STANZA deploys the image of a blacksmith as a way to figure the tiger's maker. The heat, the fortitude of the materials, and the blaze and sparks of the metalworking process paint a dramatic genesis. The pounding of hammer on anvil chimes with the driving, repetitive RHYTHM of the poem, which is shaped by TROCHAIC meter (with feet comprised of a stressed syllable followed by an unstressed syllable: ´ ˘). The insistent TONE of the poem is enhanced further by the simple scheme of RHYMING COUPLETS. The final stanza repeats the first, underscoring the urgency of the speaker's question; there is one small change—"could" shifts to "dare"—as if the meditation of the intervening stanzas has only compounded the mystery.

If the speaker's burning question concerns the creator, critics have often pursued the meaning of the tiger, many proposing that it is an ALLEGORY.

> **Research tip:** Sometimes poets address contemporary issues through the use of allegory. To explore possible allegorical meanings for the tiger, you could consult a chronology. A chronology (or timeline) gives you pertinent historical information, organized clearly by year or decade. You could search the years leading up to 1794 in *Chronology of the Modern World* or *Cassell's Chronology of World History*, for example, and find out what was going on in Blake's time. A handy, accessible online chronology is the British Library's *Timelines: Sources from History*. All of these chronologies will reveal the key historical events of the era, specifically the French Revolution (begun in 1789) and, before that, the American Revolution (begun in 1775).

It is easy to see why many critics view the tiger as an allegory for one or both of these revolutions; they were remarkable and momentous, but also violent and bloody, inspiring both awe and horror.

Another layer of the poem is revealed if we consider that Blake himself was a creator, not only as a poet but as an artist. He was a printmaker, and produced his *Songs of Innocence and Experience* as illustrated prints made from his copper engravings (look online for these striking images). A contemplation on creation, then, on both the powers of imagination and the alchemy of making, would involve personal stakes for this author. Blake could ask these questions of himself: Did I create that image? How did my hand shape that form? Where did these words come from? In this reading, the tiger is allegory for a creative work such as a poem or painting.

But let's not forget the animal. As readers we get very excited about SYMBOLS and allegories, so that sometimes we forget the so-called surface reading. Don't underestimate surfaces! A tiger is a predator of incredible beauty and power, and while it can productively signify general earthly dangers, a revolution, or creative art, it is also, itself, worthy of the speaker's awe, especially if that speaker is an eighteenth-century

Englishman encountering a live specimen. Indeed, one critic, Paul Miner, informs us that tigers were being exhibited in London during Blake's time. For hundreds of years, the Tower of London housed a menagerie that, in Blake's era, included tigers.

The enduring strength of this poem lies in its ability to yield all these competing interpretations. In turn (or all at once!), we can meditate upon the existence of God, of terror, of violent revolution, of creativity, of magnificent beasts. Innumerable other wonders and mysteries will be evoked as this poem continues to speak to new readers.

More Poems about Animals

Some questions to get you started:

"The Lamb": What differences between this poem and "The Tyger" explain their inclusion in *Songs of Innocence* and *Songs of Experience*, respectively? "The Flea": In this poem, Donne deploys the flea as a surprising, complex and extended METAPHOR we term a METAPHYSICAL CONCEIT. How does the conceit evolve as the speaker adapts to the responses of his addressee (what *is* she doing in the stanza breaks)? "A narrow Fellow in the Grass": Like "The Tyger," this poem can be read allegorically. What different ways can you interpret the figure of the snake? "A DOG": This poem comes from Gertrude Stein's 1914 collection *Tender Buttons*, a book of experimental portraits readers have found sometimes fascinating, sometimes hilarious, sometimes completely perplexing; in what ways does this odd little prose poem depict, allude to, or embody a dog? "The Shark": Without forgetting the actual shark, what else could this poem be about? "Bird-Witted": How does your reading of the title change once you have read this poem?

The Lamb

> Little lamb, who made thee?
> Dost thou know who made thee,
> Gave thee life & bid thee feed

By the stream & o'er the mead—
5 Gave thee clothing of delight,
Softest clothing, woolly bright,
Gave thee such a tender voice,
Making all the vales rejoice?
  Little lamb, who made thee,
10   Dost thou know who made thee?

  Little lamb, I'll tell thee,
  Little lamb, I'll tell thee!
He is called by thy name,
For he calls himself a Lamb;
15 He is meek & he is mild,
He became a little child:
I a child, and thou a lamb,
We are called by his name.
  Little lamb, God bless thee,
20   Little lamb, God bless thee!

      —William Blake, 1789

The Flea

Marke but this flea, and marke in this,
How little that which thou deny'st me is;
It suck'd me first, and now sucks thee,
And in this flea, our two bloods mingled bee;
5 Thou know'st that this cannot be said
A sinne, nor shame, nor losse of maidenhead,
  Yet this enjoyes before it wooe,
  And pamper'd swells with one blood made of two,
  And this, alas, is more than wee would doe.

10 Oh stay, three lives in one flea spare,
Where wee almost, yea more than maryed are.
This flea is you and I, and this
Our mariage bed, and mariage temple is;
Though parents grudge, and you, w'are met,

15 And cloysterd in these living walls of Jet.
        Though use make you apt to kill mee,
        Let not to that, selfe murder added bee,
        And sacrilege, three sinnes in killing three.

    Cruel and sodaine, hast thou since
20 Purpled thy naile, in blood of innocence?
    Wherein could this flea guilty bee,
    Except in that drop which it suckt from thee?
    Yet thou triumph'st, and saist that thou
    Find'st not thy selfe, nor mee the weaker now;
25   'Tis true, then learne how false, feares bee:
        Just so much honor, when thou yeeld'st to mee,
        Will wast, as this flea's death tooke life from thee.
                                    —John Donne, 1633

A narrow Fellow in the Grass

    A narrow Fellow in the Grass
    Occasionally rides—
    You may have met him—did you not
    His notice sudden is—

5   The Grass divides as with a Comb—
    A spotted shaft is seen—
    And then it closes at your feet
    And opens further on—

    He likes a Boggy Acre
10 A Floor too cool for Corn—
    Yet when a Boy, and Barefoot—
    I more than once at Noon

    Have passed, I thought, a Whip lash
    Unbraiding in the sun
15 When stooping to secure it
    It wrinkled, and was gone—

Several of Nature's People
I know, and they know me—
I feel for them a transport
20 Of cordiality—

But never met this Fellow,
Attended, or alone
Without a tighter breathing,
And Zero at the Bone—

                              —Emily Dickinson, 1866

A DOG

A little monkey goes like a donkey that means to say that means to
say that more sighs last goes. Leave with it. A little monkey goes like a
donkey.

                              —Gertrude Stein, 1914

The Shark

He seemed to know the harbour,
So leisurely he swam;
His fin,
Like a piece of sheet-iron,
5 Three-cornered,
And with knife-edge,
Stirred not a bubble
As it moved
With its base-line on the water.

10 His body was tubular
And tapered
And smoke-blue,
And as he passed the wharf
He turned,
15 And snapped at a flat-fish
That was dead and floating.

And I saw the flash of a white throat,
And a double row of white teeth,
And eyes of metallic grey,
20 Hard and narrow and slit.

Then out of the harbour,
With that three-cornered fin
Shearing without a bubble the water
Lithely,
25 Leisurely,
He swam—
That strange fish,
Tubular, tapered, smoke-blue,
Part vulture, part wolf,
30 Part neither—for his blood was cold.

                    —E.J. Pratt, 1923

Bird-Witted

With innocent wide penguin eyes, three
        large fledgling mocking-birds below
the pussy-willow tree,
        stand in a row,
5 wings touching, feebly solemn,
till they see
        their no longer larger
        mother bringing
something which will partially
10 feed one of them.

Toward the high-keyed intermittent squeak
        of broken carriage-springs, made by
the three similar, meek
        coated bird's-eye
15 freckled forms she comes; and when
from the beak
        of one, the still living

beetle has dropped
out, she picks it up and puts
20 it in again.

Standing in the shade till they have dressed
        their thickly-filamented, pale
pussy-willow-surfaced
        coats, they spread tail
25 and wings, showing one by one,
the modest
        white stripe lengthwise on the
        tail and crosswise
underneath the wing, and the
30 accordion

is closed again. What delightful note
        with rapid unexpected flute-
sounds leaping from the throat
        of the astute
35 grown bird, comes back to one from
the remote
        unenergetic sun-
        lit air before
the brood was here? How harsh
40 the bird's voice has become.

A piebald cat observing them,
        is slowly creeping toward the trim
trio on the tree-stem.
        Unused to him
45 the three make room—uneasy
new problem.
        A dangling foot that missed
        its grasp, is raised
and finds the twig on which it
50 planned to perch. The

parent darting down, nerved by what chills
    the blood, and by hope rewarded—
of toil—since nothing fills
    squeaking unfed
55 mouths, wages deadly combat,
and half kills
    with bayonet beak and
    cruel wings, the
intellectual cautious-
60 ly c r e e p ing cat.

                      —Marianne Moore, 1936

Poem Discussion Seven

r-p-o-p-h-e-s-s-a-g-r, by E.E. Cummings

                    r-p-o-p-h-e-s-s-a-g-r
              who
      a)s w(e loo)k
      upnowgath
              PPEGORHRASS
                              eringint(o-
      aThe):l
            eA
              !p:
      S   a
              (r
      rIvInG   .gRrEaPsPhOs)
                                    to
      rea(be)rran(com)gi(e)ngly
      ,grasshopper;

                                    —1932

IF YOU FIND THE poem above makes absolutely no sense, lucky you! Although in future this poem will continue to delight you, you will never again have the experience of initial bewilderment that makes for "r-p-o-p-h-e-s-s-a-g-r"'s most dramatic blooming. So stop reading this paragraph right now, and spend a few more minutes figuring out how to read E.E. Cummings's (1894–1962) poem.

Whether students embrace or resent the puzzlement they feel during their first encounter with this CONCRETE poem, ten minutes later they are all at least tickled by what they've unravelled. You might have picked out some variation on "grasshopper who (as we look up) now, gathering into a grasshopper, leaps! The grasshopper arriving to become (rearrangingly) grasshopper." This rearrangement of the text into more standard sentences produces a passage that evocatively describes the shifting limbs and appendages of a grasshopper as it fulfils the promise of its name in leaping, and then resettles in the grass. That it would "become" itself also evokes the perceiver's experience of noticing the insect only as it launches into view.

But, importantly, the poem is not presented in standard sentences. So while the transcription of the scrambled letters above yields a compelling statement, the real energy of the poem is activated in the process of your reading. As your eyes bounce here and there, piecing syllables together and leaping from letter to letter, you perform a kind of embodiment of the leaping insect.

In concrete poetry, shape is important, but we don't get here a poem in the shape of a grasshopper; instead the poem's unusual arrangement enacts a choreography of both the insect's movement and, more subtly, a perceiver's recognition of that insect as it makes itself known in momentary flight.

One of the wonderful things about this poem is the way it highlights the agency of the reader. The embodiment of the grasshopper occurs in the moment of your active engagement with the text. You perform this poem. Try doodling the flight path of your eyes as they track the letters in the poem. When I do this there's a huge loop in the middle, around the airy "leA!p:S"; the dynamic movement of the reader's eyes coincides with the most dramatic moment of the grasshopper's dance. The loop is caused in part by the odd beginning of line 7, the articles "a" and "The" fused together. The juxtaposition of indefinite and definite articles echoes nicely the themes of becoming, of vagueness and visibility, of there and not there, in this piece. Your reading might place "a grasshopper" before "The grasshopper" or you might put them the other way around. Either way, the eye does a loop-de-loop.

Or your phrasing might introduce the leap with an article, as in "gathering into a (or The) leap!" Each of your own encounters with this poem will be slightly different. The poem is arranged in such a way as to preclude the definite 'solution' to a puzzle. The poem isn't used up once you've read it the first time. In the glossary to this book you'll see that STANZA, in Italian, means "room." I think of that meaning when I consider Cummings's poem. This poem is a single stanza, a room I like to enter again and again, and each time I notice different features, and enjoy a different experience.

No matter how I read this poem, there always remains a surplus of punctuation marks—hyphens, parentheses, semicolons, etc.—that don't fit into the reconstructed phrases. Perhaps these marks whimsically represent eyes, antennae, feet, blades of grass? There are lots of formal details to investigate: Why mix capitals and small letters? Why do the "S" and "a" exceed the boundaries of the poem (a feature Cummings insisted on in notes to a publisher)?

Like all good concrete poetry, "r-p-o-p-h-e-s-s-a-g-r" reconnects us with the material that is language. The unusual organization of letters here forces us to slow down, to notice the micro elements of text. We are also invited to attend to the micro events in the natural world, the magnificent small moment of the grasshopper's jump. After reading this poem, you might find the letters of the next thing you read (even if it's a newspaper!) leaping out at you.

More Concrete Poems

Some questions to get you started:

"Easter Wings": How do the contours of Herbert's poem signify in more than one way? "l(a": How does this Cummings poem, like "r-p-o-p-h-e-s-s-a-g-r," both describe and embody, through the performance of the reader? "Forsythia": Look carefully at the marks linking letters to comprise the branches of this bush; what are these dots and dashes and how do they contribute to the poem's effect? "Cycle No. 22": Sound poetry is a form of concrete poetry which highlights the sonic resources of language; read this poem aloud or listen to bp Nichol read it at www.bpnichol.ca. What do you hear in the cycled phrase "drum and a wheel"? "In Medias Res": How does the structure of McFee's sentence resonate with the poem's shape? "Love Song": How does Christakos's poem animate the meaning-making function of space and shape?

Easter Wings

Lord, who createdst man in wealth and store,°   *abundance*
Though foolishly he lost the same,
Decaying more and more,
Till he became
Most poore:
With thee
O let me rise
As larks, harmoniously,
And sing this day thy victories:
Then shall the fall further the flight in me.

My tender age in sorrow did beginne:
And still with sicknesses and shame
Thou didst so punish sinne,
That I became
Most thinne.
With thee
Let me combine,
And feel thy victorie:
For, if I imp° my wing on thine,   *graft*
Affliction shall advance the flight in me.

—George Herbert, 1633

l(a

le
af
fa

ll

s)
one
l

iness

—E.E. Cummings, 1958

Forsythia

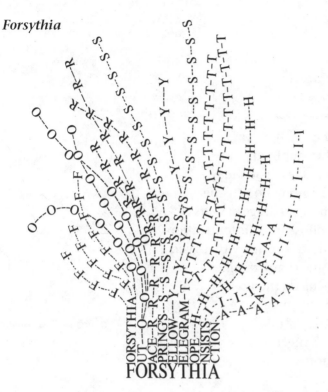

—Mary Ellen Solt, 1965

Cycle No. 22

VERSION EXECUTED MAY 6/80
ORATOR TYPEFACE ON IBM SELECTRIC

—bp Nichol, 1980

In Medias Res[1]

His waist,
like the plot,
thickens, wedding
pants now breathtaking,
belt no longer the cinch
it once was, belly's cambium[2]
expanding to match each birthday,
his body a wad of anonymous tissue
swung in the same centrifuge of years
that separates a house from its foundation,
undermining sidewalks grim with joggers
and loose-filled graves and families
and stars collapsing on themselves,
no preservation society capable
of plugging entropy's° dike,   *degradation, disorder*
under the zipper's sneer
a belly hibernation-
soft, ready for
the kill.

—Michael McFee, 1996

Love Song

in u
i nu

—Margaret Christakos, 2013

---

1   *In Medias Res*: Latin. Literary term referring to practice of commencing a narrative "in
      the midst of things."
2   *cambium*: Growth layer in plants, forms annual tree rings.

Poem Discussion Eight

Daddy, by Sylvia Plath

Daddy

You do not do, you do not do
Any more, black shoe
In which I have lived like a foot
For thirty years, poor and white,
5 Barely daring to breathe or Achoo.

Daddy, I have had to kill you.
You died before I had time—
Marble-heavy, a bag full of God,
Ghastly statue with one grey toe
10 Big as a Frisco° seal   *San Francisco*

And a head in the freakish Atlantic
Where it pours bean green over blue
In the waters off beautiful Nauset.°   *Cape Cod beach*
I used to pray to recover you.
15 Ach, du.°   *(German) Oh, you*

In the German tongue, in the Polish town
Scraped flat by the roller
Of wars, wars, wars.
But the name of the town is common.
20 My Polack friend

Says there are a dozen or two.
So I never could tell where you
Put your foot, your root,

I never could talk to you.
25   The tongue stuck in my jaw.

It stuck in a barb wire snare.
Ich,° ich, ich, ich,   *(German) I*
I could hardly speak.
I thought every German was you.
30   And the language obscene

An engine, an engine
Chuffing me off like a Jew.
A Jew to Dachau, Auschwitz, Belsen.[1]
I began to talk like a Jew.
35   I think I may well be a Jew.

The snows of the Tyrol,[2] the clear beer of Vienna
Are not very pure or true.
With my gypsy ancestress and my weird luck
And my Taroc pack and my Taroc pack
40   I may be a bit of a Jew.

I have always been scared of *you*,
With your Luftwaffe,° your gobbledygoo.   *air force of Nazi Germany*
And your neat mustache
And your Aryan eye, bright blue.
45   Panzer°-man, panzer-man, O You—   *World War II German tank*

Not God but a swastika
So black no sky could squeak through.
Every woman adores a Fascist,
The boot in the face, the brute
50   Brute heart of a brute like you.

You stand at the blackboard, daddy,
In the picture I have of you,

1   *Dachau, Auschwitz, Belsen*: Sites of Nazi concentration camps.
2   *Tyrol*: Alpine region straddling Austria and northern Italy.

A cleft in your chin instead of your foot
But no less a devil for that, no not
55   Any less the black man who

Bit my pretty red heart in two.
I was ten when they buried you.
At twenty I tried to die
And get back, back, back to you.
60   I thought even the bones would do.

But they pulled me out of the sack,
And they stuck me together with glue.
And then I knew what to do.
I made a model of you,
65   A man in black with a Meinkampf[1] look

And a love of the rack and the screw.
And I said I do, I do.
So daddy, I'm finally through.
The black telephone's off at the root,
70   The voices just can't worm through.

If I've killed one man, I've killed two—
The vampire who said he was you
And drank my blood for a year,
Seven years, if you want to know.
75   Daddy, you can lie back now.

There's a stake in your fat black heart
And the villagers never liked you.
They are dancing and stamping on you.
They always *knew* it was you.
80   Daddy, daddy, you bastard, I'm through.

—1965

---

1   *Mein Kampf:* (*My Struggle*) Adolf Hitler's autobiography.

WHILE THIS POEM ADDRESSES a "you," we wouldn't call it an ODE; rather than a formal, laudatory APOSTROPHE, Sylvia Plath (1932–63) has written a tortured indictment whose tonal landscape of frustration, anger and grief make it one of the most memorable, emotionally harrowing poems of the twentieth century. When "Daddy" is on my course syllabus, it is unfailingly the poem which elicits the most passionate response in students. Let's think about how Plath has constructed "Daddy," a work that continues to move readers decades after she wrote it.

In the first STANZA we can already see the forces of sound and IMAGERY which contribute so profoundly to the power of this poem. The primary image here is presented as a SIMILE; the SPEAKER is like a foot encased in the shoe that is her father. What is suggested by this simile? A foot is bound, imprisoned by the shoe, an oppressive dynamic underscored here by the speaker's "Barely daring to breathe or Achoo." The black shoe shadows, or blots out, the bloodless white foot, anticipating the vampiric imagery at the end of the poem. Yet a shoe is inanimate, and a foot alive; the poem is, in part, a pained attempt to achieve release from the dead parent's memory.

You probably noticed the ASSONANCE in the first line: every word of "You do not do, you do not do" features an 'ooh' sound, a sound repeated in "shoe," "poor," "to," and "Achoo." Moving on through the poem, words ending with the 'ooh' sound comprise the dominant set of END RHYMES. Sixteen lines terminate with "you," for example. (What does the preponderance of the word "you" suggest about the success of the speaker's attempt at exorcism?) Plath's heavy use of assonance raises the question of how it contributes to the tone of the poem. Do sounds carry with them moods, tones, associations? This is debatable, of course, but I can't help but compare the pursed-mouth effort it takes to speak Plath's first line with the open, dreamy effect of Phyllis Webb's assonant phrase "Ah—to have a name like *Wah*" ("Sunday Water" 12).

The word "Achoo" is odd, and particularly odd as a verb. Its placement in the first stanza prepares us for the recurrence of childlike DICTION in the poem; we will see "gobbledygoo," excessive repetition, the choice of "Daddy" rather than "Dad" or "Father," and childlike constructions such as "They are dancing and stamping on you." Why does an adult speaker express herself this way? In stanza twelve we learn that the speaker was ten when her father died. So while the speaker is mature, much of the pain she expresses originates in a trauma experienced in childhood. This feature of juvenile diction strikes many of my students as psychologically realistic, conveying the original loss and betraying unresolved grief in the adult.

Stanzas two and three establish an emotional landscape replete with contradiction. The speaker claims an act of violence against her father, with "I have had to kill you," then remembers, "I used to pray to recover you." Anger, desire, and grief intermingle. How do you read that dash, then, at the end of line 7?:

Daddy, I have had to kill you.
You died before I had time—

The phrase is incomplete. Time for what? The dash leaves the possibilities open. The previous line prompts us to complete the phrase with "to kill you," which is consonant with the vengeful strain in the poem. But you could also complete the phrase with "to know you well, to experience a full relationship with my father," a sentiment chiming with the poem's poignant notes of loss. In addition to accommodating the tonal reach of the poem, the dash is important because it marks a silence, manifesting both the impossibility of expressing the inexpressible and the particular frustration of communication thematized in "Daddy."

The images following the dash convey the space the father occupies in the speaker's psyche. He is described in monumental terms, as "Marble-heavy, a bag full of God." Plath uses the image of a statue straddling the continent to illustrate his imposing presence, "with one gray toe / Big as a Frisco seal / And a head in the freakish Atlantic." Not only would a parent's early death colonize the continent of a child's mind, but generally it takes a lot of growing up before we can view our parents as mere humans. In a note on the poem, Plath describes her speaker as someone who had lost a parent "while she thought he was God" ("Script for the BBC" 196).

While in that note Plath refers to the speaker of "Daddy" in the third person, much discussion of this famous poem concerns its autobiographical resonance. Plath has been placed in a grouping of poets known as **CONFESSIONAL POETS**, the term 'confessional' coined in a 1959 review by critic M.L. Rosenthal to indicate work exhibiting an unprecedented level of emotional honesty and personal revelation. We are careful as critics not to conflate writer and narrator, or poet and speaker, but in confessional poetry the line is especially blurry. Plath's father, Otto Plath, did die when she was a little girl, from complications after a leg amputation necessitated by untreated diabetes. The crisis began with a gangrenous toe, lending extra gravity to that image of the "one gray toe" in line 9. Otto was born in the Polish Corridor of Germany, and Plath's mother, Aurelia, had Austrian roots, both features of ancestry articulated in the poem. The second major figure in the poem, the "model of you," we can easily connect with Ted Hughes (1930–98), the father of Plath's two very young children and partner for the seven years mentioned in the poem. Hughes left Plath for another woman in September of 1962, and "Daddy" was written in October—October 12th, to be exact, the anniversary of her father's amputation.

  In the case of "Daddy," then, biographical research does add a meaningful dimension to our analysis. But even in this case, there remains a distance between author and speaker. While a poet's life experience necessarily informs their creative work, that work is a new entity, an object enriched by the artistic transmutation of experience. We can see a minor illustration of this distance in line 57: "I was ten when they buried you." Plath was eight when her father died, but a poignant symmetry is achieved by the juxtaposition of loss at ten and a suicide attempt at twenty. That Plath's goal is a powerful expression of emotional truth rather than a factually accurate account is most clear in her deployment of Holocaust imagery to figure the dynamic between father and daughter.

  Otto Plath was not a Nazi, nor was Sylvia Plath Jewish. Yet she chooses this historical genocide as **METAPHOR** through which to figure the speaker's agony. Her choice ignited massive debate amongst critics and readers. Many saw the metaphor as highly offensive, a diminishing of the overwhelming horror of the Holocaust. Some saw the move as a profound linking of public and private wounds. Critic George Steiner noted that Plath was one of the few writers mentioning the

Holocaust at a time when the world was still mostly silent about what had happened to the Jews in World War II. My students have offered lots of thoughtful opinions on the issue. I've heard the argument that the imagery is irresponsible, and ruins the poem. I've heard the argument that only through invoking that level of horror could one convey a child's grief. One student proposed that Plath might have been ambivalent about the imagery as well—that we should remember it is meant to issue from the constructed psyche of the speaker, not Plath. Responses vary among readers and have certainly shifted over the decades since the poem's composition. How did you respond to the imagery when you read it?

The Nazi imagery arises out of the speaker's frustrated communication with her father. The impenetrable veil between life and death is strikingly depicted as linguistic struggle, the child unable to converse in the German mothertongue of her father. The line "The tongue stuck in my jaw" stands out; why "The tongue" rather than *my* tongue? Something as minute as the choice of article can signify much. One thing "The" allows is a double meaning: the tongue can refer to the German language as well as the organ of speech. But if we consider the organ, introducing it with "The" rather than "my" also suggests the speaker's dissociation from her own body, in particular her own vehicle of expression. Being unable to locate and communicate with the father sparks a crisis in her own self-knowledge. Fittingly, it is the German word for "I" she contends with in line 27: "Ich, ich, ich, ich." The CONSONANCE—in this case repeated German [ç] sounds—in that line makes it very challenging for English speakers, so that here again we find Plath deploying the power of sound to colour an utterance, in this case an anguished articulation of self.

As the emotional pitch in the work escalates, we encounter more repetition, in "the brute / Brute heart of a brute like you." This phrase performs the inarticulateness of a child or a person who is extremely upset, or both. Just a few lines before this there appears the poem's second dash, at the end of the ninth stanza: "Panzer-man, panzer-man, O You—." The silence of that dash is loud in its frustration. The dash might also stand in for profanity; note that by the end of the poem the speaker can say "you bastard." Jacqueline Rose has made the interesting observation that in calling her father a bastard, the speaker renders him, like her, fatherless. No other epithet could be as resonant. This astute reading illustrates the artistry behind every word in Plath's poem—and exemplifies, as well, the revelations you yourself can offer when you read attentively.

The final few stanzas of the poem shift focus to the reincarnation of the father, the second man to abandon the speaker. Here the two figures fuse in the figure of the vampire, so when the speaker declares "There's a stake in your fat black heart," she could be talking about both men. The reference to her marriage vows—"And I said I do, I do"—echoes the poem's opening line, raising the possibility that the "You" who "do not do" could be double. It's always interesting to see how the conclusion of a poem inflects its beginning.

> **Research tip:** Another element inflecting meaning is context. That is, reading a poem in the context of a book of the poet's work is often a different experience from reading it in a literary journal or anthology. The poem can echo, build upon, oppose, or complicate features of the poems around it in ways that affect meaning-making. In the case of "Daddy," context is a particularly fascinating consideration. The poem appeared in *Ariel* (1965), a collection of Plath's poems that Ted Hughes published after her death by suicide. But the poems included in that collection did not match the table of contents Plath had planned. The poet's *Collected Poems* came out in 1981 and included in its notes Plath's original list, which inspired critics to consider how the two *Ariel* manuscripts differ. Marjorie Perloff's article, "The Two Ariels: The (Re)making of the Sylvia Plath Canon" (1984), offers a compelling discussion of how "Daddy" signifies quite differently when read within the book Plath designed. Perloff persuasively demonstrates that within its original context "Daddy" reads primarily as "a cry of outrage against the deceiving husband" (15). Since then a new edition has appeared, *Ariel: The Restored Edition* (2004); there you can see a facsimile of Plath's original manuscript.

The poem ends on "through," a word appearing three times in the final stanzas and emblematizing in its multiple meanings the tonal complexity of this finale. At once we hear triumph, bitterness, bravado, and defeat. That "The black telephone's off at the root, / The voices just can't worm through" intimates the completion of the speaker's exorcism; neither man can reach or affect her now. But in the vein of that theme of communication, we can read the preceding line, "So daddy, I'm finally through," as a declaration that she has achieved connection. To be "through" is to be "done with," so we can also interpret the claim as an announcement that the speaker is over her fixations and can move on now. Read more negatively, to be "through" is to be conquered, to give up. Knowing that Sylvia Plath committed suicide just four months after composing this work can lend an especially tragic note to her final statement, "I'm through."

While communication between the speaker and her addressees is vexed or broken, that between Plath and her audience is rich and vivid. In my discussion of "Daddy" I keep returning to the elements of sound (such as assonance, repetition and diction) that distinguish this powerful LYRIC poem which speaks to so many readers. While 'lyric' now indicates any short poem featuring a single expressive voice, the sonic potency of "Daddy" points to the ancient sense of the term, indicating a song to be accompanied by a lyre. Plath said of a group of poems written in 1962, including "Daddy": "they are written for the ear, not the eye: they are poems written out loud" ("Script for the BBC" 195).

More Poems "for the ear"

Some questions to get you started:

"Jabberwocky": This poem is full of NEOLOGISMS (made up words); how do they mean? (Note: "galumphing" and "chortled" were nonsense in 1871, but were so evocative we've now adopted them!) "God's Grandeur": Poets generally avoid starting a word with the same sound the preceding word ended with; why does Hopkins stage this awkward meeting twice in line 7? "at the cemetery, walnut grove plantation, south carolina, 1989": How does repetition contribute to the power of this FREE VERSE poem? "Zong! #1": This is the first poem in a book Philip describes as a "Song of the untold story" of 150 slaves thrown overboard off the slaveship *Zong* in 1871. What is the effect of breaking words down into sounds here? You can go to the University of Pennsylvania's Pennsound website to hear a recording (writing. upenn.edu/pennsound/x/Philip.php). "Ravine": What role do assonance and consonance play in this poem's buzz?

Jabberwocky

'Twas brillig, and the slithy toves
    Did gyre and gimble in the wabe;
All mimsy were the borogoves,
    And the mome raths outgrabe.

5 "Beware the Jabberwock, my son!
    The jaws that bite, the claws that catch!
Beware the Jubjub bird, and shun
    The frumious Bandersnatch!"

He took his vorpal sword in hand;
10   Long time the manxome foe he sought—
So rested he by the Tumtum tree
    And stood awhile in thought.

And, as in uffish thought he stood,
    The Jabberwock, with eyes of flame,
15 Came whiffling through the tulgey wood,
    And burbled as it came!

One, two! One, two! And through and through
    The vorpal blade went snicker-snack!
He left it dead, and with its head
20   He went galumphing back.

"And hast thou slain the Jabberwock?
    Come to my arms, my beamish boy!
O frabjous day! Callooh! Callay!"
    He chortled in his joy.

25 'Twas brillig, and the slithy toves
        Did gyre and gimble in the wabe;
      All mimsy were the borogoves,
        And the mome raths outgrabe.

                        —Lewis Carroll, 1871

God's Grandeur

      The world is charged with the grandeur of God.
        It will flame out, like shining from shook foil;
        It gathers to a greatness, like the ooze of oil
      Crushed. Why do men then now not reck his rod?°
5   Generations have trod, have trod, have trod;   *heed his law*
        And all is seared with trade; bleared, smeared with toil;
        And wears man's smudge and shares man's smell: the soil
      Is bare now, nor can foot feel, being shod.°

                                                                  wearing shoes

      And for all this, nature is never spent;
10   There lives the dearest freshness deep down things;
      And though the last lights off the black West went
        Oh, morning, at the brown brink eastward, springs—
      Because the Holy Ghost over the bent
        World broods with warm breast and with ah! bright wings.

                        —Gerard Manley Hopkins (1918)

at the cemetery,
walnut grove plantation, south carolina, 1989

      among the rocks
      at walnut grove
      your silence drumming
      in my bones,
5   tell me your names.

      nobody mentioned slaves
      and yet the curious tools
      shine with your fingerprints.

nobody mentioned slaves
10 but somebody did this work
who had no guide, no stone,
who moulders under rock.

tell me your names,
tell me your bashful names
15 and i will testify.

the inventory lists ten slaves
but only men were recognized.

among the rocks
at walnut grove
20 some of these honored dead
were dark
some of these dark
were slaves
some of these slaves
25 were women
some of them did this
honored work.
tell me your names
foremothers, brothers,
30 tell me your dishonored names.
here lies
here lies
here lies
here lies
35 hear

—Lucille Clifton, 1991

Zong! #1

    w w w   w   a wa

        w   a   w a   t

er   wa   s

    our   wa

te r gg   g   g   go

    o   oo   goo   d

    waa   wa wa

w w waa

    ter   o   oh

on   o   ne   w one

    w o n   d d d

    ey   d   a

dey   a ah   ay

    s   one   day s

    wa   wa

Masuz Zuwena Ogunsheye Ziyad Ogwambi Keturah

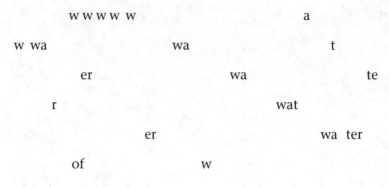

w w w w w   a

w wa   wa   t

er   wa   te

r   wat

er   wa ter

of   w

ant

―――――――――――
Aba Chimanga Naeema Oba Eshe

—M. NourbeSe Philip, 2008

Ravine

Glee bee
bumble
rumble bee
be!

5 Pepperfilled thimble
glee bee
bumble
rumbles be.

Glee on the edge, ravine
10 looks over ravine
ravine oh bee
ravine mad

glee bee
bumble
15 rumble bee be
bee ravine mad about ravine.

Ravine bee.
Bee ravine.
Ravine glee
20 bee bumble rumble

be!
Pepperfilled thimble sprinkle
bee ravine
glee.

25 Glee on the edge, ravine
glee on the edge, ravine glee
on the edge ravine
bee.

—Louis Cabri, 2014

Poem Discussion Nine

kitchenette building, by Gwendolyn Brooks

to David and Keziah Brooks

kitchenette building

We are things of dry hours and the involuntary plan,
Grayed in, and gray. "Dream" makes a giddy sound, not strong
Like "rent," "feeding a wife," "satisfying a man."

But could a dream send up through onion fumes
5 Its white and violet, fight with fried potatoes
And yesterday's garbage ripening in the hall,
Flutter, or sing an aria down these rooms

Even if we were willing to let it in,
Had time to warm it, keep it very clean,
10 Anticipate a message, let it begin?

We wonder. But not well! not for a minute!
Since Number Five is out of the bathroom now,
We think of lukewarm water, hope to get in it.

—1945

A FIRST READ THROUGH THIS poem reveals that its setting is of prime importance. This calls for some research into the nature of a "kitchenette building."

One of the first things you might notice about the poem is its pronoun. Instead of using the traditional LYRIC "I", the SPEAKER voices a "we." How does this choice contribute to the portrait in this work? Well, it might emphasize the lack of privacy depicted in the poem, the lack of solitude one needs for the ruminative development of a "dream," the focal image of the poem. At the same time, however, a "we" can announce community, a dynamic of solidarity rather than conflict. Like Plath, Brooks manages to create a tonal landscape rich with overlapping, even competing, possibilities.

> **Research tip:** Look to two of the scholarly resources you've learned about: After discovering in a biography (see Research Tip on p. 18) that Gwendolyn Brooks (1917–2000) was based in Chicago, you could search for information on kitchenette buildings in a subject encyclopedia (see Research Tip on p. 26). *The Electronic Encyclopedia of Chicago*, an online source, offers an entry on kitchenettes. The entry describes the practice, during the early to mid-twentieth century, of subdividing existing housing into tiny living units. Rented primarily to African Americans, the apartments were cramped and ill-equipped: "Entire families occupied single rooms, sharing with other residents an inadequate number of bathrooms and kitchens, exceeding the plumbing capacity, and leading to a serious deterioration in sanitary conditions. During the 1940s, more than 80,000 conversions of this type had occurred in Chicago, leading to a 52 percent increase in units lacking private bath facilities" (Plotkin). Gathering this historical knowledge enriches your understanding of Brooks's powerful poem.

The language in the first sentence establishes the circumstances of the communal we. Strikingly, these people are "things," objects rather than subjects. Their hours are "dry," not an adjective that implies time devoted to stimulating experiences and fruitful creative endeavours. The "involuntary plan" characterizes life trajectories as beyond their control, and points toward the central critique of this poem, that of the American Dream. The American Dream would suggest that anyone willing to work hard can achieve success, regardless of race, class, religion, etc. But for the speaker, "'Dream' makes a giddy sound;" it's a frivolous notion necessarily taking a back seat to the more practical and pressing obligations of survival, such as making rent. The repetition in "Grayed in, and gray" declares the reason. The phrase speaks to the connection between environment and identity;

this community is hemmed in by, and thus becomes, "gray." The portrait in this work declares that circumstances play a large role in determining potential. How far can hard work take you without the supports of financial investment, adequate housing, education, and health care?

We've talked a lot in this book about literary devices, the meaning-making forces of tools such as ALLITERATION, METAPHOR, and METER. I want to address "kitchenette building" because it illustrates the role plain old SYNTAX plays in poetic works. Thinking about grammar, about how phrases and sentences are organized, is key to investigating the power of poetry. Take a close look at the second STANZA of the poem. A number of clauses begin to pile up. Digging out the central thread, you can isolate "But could a dream send up ... / Its white and violet, ... / Flutter, or sing an aria." This heavenly proposition is interrupted by "through onion fumes" and then "fight with fried potatoes / And yesterday's garbage ripening in the hall." Through this syntactical arrangement, Brooks is able to demonstrate the impediments to dreaming, the waylaid phrase evoking the frustrated dreams and ambitions of the kitchenette's inhabitants. That the second stanza is the only one with four lines serves to emphasize the obstacles. The sentence continues on into the third stanza, which proceeds to raise more doubts about the viability of a dream in such a setting.

The fourth stanza begins with "We wonder," a phrase which seems to refer to the vexed question posed by the previous two stanzas. Wondering is something like dreaming; so they are dreaming—but only about the possibility of dreaming! This suggests once again the fugitive quality of any fully elaborated plan, dream or ambition. The period after "wonder" delivers a CAESURA, a startling mid-line stop which effectively underscores the lost cause of dreaming. We are told the speaker can't wonder "well! not for a minute!", but that message is most dramatically communicated through the caesura, which puts a stop to wondering.

The poem ends by bringing us resolutely into the mundane, practical concerns of survival. The neighbours are referred to as "Number Five," a dehumanizing title recalling the "things" of line 1. And the fleeting notion of an otherworldly dream is now deflated to the thought of a tepid bath in the shared bathroom. The bathos (sorry for the pun!) of the final image is emphasized by the decidedly unromantic, almost humorous, RHYME of "not for a minute!" with "hope to get in it."

Tracing the rhyme scheme of the poem, you'll find that the first and last lines of each stanza rhyme, making the poem loosely reminiscent of a traditional TERZA RIMA. The meter is also evocative of IAMBIC PENTAMETER, with line 9—"Had time to warm it, keep it very clean"—adhering precisely. This play with traditional form is typical of much of Brooks's work; she ingeniously reworks received modes to fulfil her own poetic vision. In the case of "kitchenette building," the tension between regular form and more organic expression helps convey the thematic tension between dream and reality. This is not exactly to say, though, that the dream would be perfectly embodied by regular form, and that deviations from the traditional coincide with the dream's failure. It is, for example, the chaos of the stanza overfull with interfering clauses and the humour of the banal final words which make for the original and unique music of the poem. The poem itself does "Flutter"; it is "an aria." In the end, we are left with a work which conveys devastating truths about poverty while imbuing a portrait of hopelessness with a glimmer of hope.

More Poems Displaying the Poetic Force of Syntax

Some questions to get you started:

"When I Heard the Learn'd Astronomer": What is conveyed by the successive, ever-lengthening clauses in the first four lines? "In a Station of the Metro": What is the effect of Pound's choice to give us two verbless phrases, linked by a semi-colon? "ASPARAGUS": Can this portrait of asparagus do something a syntactically normal description can't? "since feeling is first": Ironically, Cummings *does* attend to syntax here; how is it orchestrated to project a speaker for whom "feeling is first"? "Rolling Motion": How are parts of speech put into uncommon service to create this erotic scene? "monday": How do syntactical patterns drive the structure of this poem? "Winter": How does this poem tune you in to grammar?

When I Heard the Learn'd Astronomer

When I heard the learn'd astronomer,
When the proofs, the figures, were ranged in columns before me,
When I was shown the charts and diagrams, to add, divide, and
       measure them,
When I sitting heard the astronomer where he lectured with much
       applause in the lecture-room,
5 How soon unaccountable I became tired and sick,
Till rising and gliding out I wander'd off by myself,
In the mystical moist night-air, and from time to time,
Look'd up in perfect silence at the stars.

                  —Walt Whitman, 1865

In a Station of the Metro

The apparition of these faces in the crowd;
Petals on a wet, black bough.

                  —Ezra Pound, 1913

ASPARAGUS

Asparagus in a lean in a lean to hot. This makes it art and it is wet wet
weather wet weather wet.

                  —Gertrude Stein, 1914

since feeling is first

since feeling is first
who pays any attention
to the syntax of things
will never wholly kiss you;

5 wholly to be a fool
while Spring is in the world

my blood approves,
and kisses are a better fate
than wisdom
10   lady i swear by all flowers. Don't cry
—the best gesture of my brain is less than
your eyelids' flutter which says

we are for each other: then
laugh, leaning back in my arms
15   for life's not a paragraph

And death i think is no parenthesis

—E.E. Cummings, 1927

Rolling Motion

Your face in my neck &
arms dwelling upward face
in my soft leg open
lifted upward airborne soft
5   face into under into rolling
over every upward motion
rolling open over your
Face in my neck again over
turning risen touch billows
10   my mouth open enter
dwelling upward face
in your soft leg open
lifted upward airborne soft
face into under into motion
15   over every upward open
rolling open over your
Face in my neck again
& arms

—Erin Mouré, 1988

monday (from *the weather*)

First all belief is paradise. So pliable a medium. A time
not very long. A transparency caused. A conveyance of
rupture. A subtle transport. Scant and rare. Deep in the
opulent morning, blissful regions, hard and slender.
5 Scarce and scant. Quotidian and temperate. Begin afresh
in the realms of the atmosphere, that encompasses the
solid earth, the terraqueous globe that soars and sings,
elevated and flimsy. Bright and hot. Flesh and hue. Our
skies are inventions, durations, discoveries, quotas, forg-
10 eries, fine and grand. Fine and grand. Fresh and bright.
Heavenly and bright. The day pours out space, a light red
roominess, bright and fresh. Bright and oft. Bright and
fresh. Sparkling and wet. Clamour and tint. We range the
spacious fields, a battlement trick and fast. Bright and
15 silver. Ribbons and failings. To and fro. Fine and grand.
The sky is complicated and flawed and we're up there in it,
floating near the apricot frill, the bias swoop, near the
sullen bloated part that dissolves to silver the next instant
bronze but nothing that meaningful, a breach of greeny-
20 blue, a syllable, we're all across the swathe of fleece laid
out, the fraying rope, the copper beech behind the
aluminum catalpa that has saved the entire spring for this
flight, the tops of these a part of the sky, the light wind
flipping up the white undersides of leaves, heaven afresh,
25 the brushed part behind, the tumbling. So to the heavenly
rustling. Just stiff with ambition we range the spacious
trees in earnest desire sure and dear. Brisk and west.
Streaky and massed. Changing and appearing. First and
last. This was made from Europe, formed from Europe,
30 rant and roar. Fine and grand. Fresh and bright. Crested
and turbid. Silver and bright. This was spoken as it came
to us, to celebrate and tint, distinct and designed. Sure and
dear. Fully designed. Dear afresh. So free to the showing.
What we praise we believe, we fully believe. Very fine.
35 Belief thin and pure and clear to the title. Very beautiful.

Belief lovely and elegant and fair for the footing. Very
brisk. Belief lively and quick and strong by the bursting.
Very bright. Belief clear and witty and famous in impulse.
Very stormy. Belief violent and open and raging from
40 privation. Very fine. Belief intransigent after pursuit. Very
hot. Belief lustful and eager and curious before beauty.
Very bright. Belief intending afresh. So calmly and clearly.
Just stiff with leaf sure and dear and appearing and last.
With lust clear and scarce and appearing and last and
45 afresh.

—Lisa Robertson, 2001

Winter

Knowing he's dead, Glenn Gould plays Schoenberg.
Knowing he's dead, Glenn Gould plays Schoenberg.

—Mark Truscott, 2004

Poem Discussion Ten

The Three Emilys, by Dorothy Livesay

The Three Emilys *

These women crying in my head
Walk alone, uncomforted:
The Emilys, these three
Cry to be set free—
5   And others whom I will not name
Each different, each the same.

Yet they had liberty!
Their kingdom was the sky:
They batted clouds with easy hand,
10 Found a mountain for their stand;
From wandering lonely they could catch
The inner magic of a heath—
A lake their palette, any tree
Their brush could be.

15 And still they cry to me
As in reproach—
I, born to hear their inner storm
Of separate man in woman's form,
I yet possess another kingdom, barred
20 To them, these three, this Emily.
I move as mother in a frame,
My arteries
Flow the immemorial way
Towards the child, the man;
25 And only for brief span

Am I an Emily on mountain snows
And one of these.

And so the whole that I possess
Is still much less—
30   They move triumphant through my head:
I am the one
Uncomforted.

*Emily Brontë, Emily Dickinson, and Emily Carr.

—1953

MANY OF THE POEMS we've looked at invite us to attend more closely to our world, and to critique social injustices found there. "Harlem Dancer," for example, questioned both the objectification of women and racially coded standards of beauty. "kitchenette building" asked us to reflect on myths about poverty. In "The Three Emilys," Dorothy Livesay (1909–96) addresses the dilemma of the woman artist.

STANZA one introduces the three figures "crying" in the SPEAKER's head: Emily Brontë (British novelist, 1818–48), Emily Dickinson (American poet, 1830–86) and Emily Carr (Canadian painter and writer, 1871–1945). In the mind of the speaker, these famous women "Walk alone, uncomforted" and "Cry to be set free—." Free from what? In what ways are they "each the same"? What they all have in common is achievement, fame (even if posthumous), and lives led outside the norm of marriage and childbearing. We know that in the third stanza the speaker reveals her own position as wife and mother, so it appears she may be sympathizing with women who lacked spouse and children, imagining they craved freedom from isolation.

The second stanza contradicts the first, expounding on the "liberty" of the Emilys. The HYPERBOLE of lines 8–9 conveys the speaker's sense of their boundless freedom and titanic stature as artists: "Their kingdom was the sky: / They batted clouds with easy hand." Here are women whose creative lives were unhindered by the principal duties, responsibilities, and expectations associated with 'proper' womanhood (i.e., marriage and motherhood) in their times. The natural IMAGERY continues in the stanza, the speaker claiming that in their "wandering lonely" the three Emilys could harness the beauty and creative powers of Nature. The natural imagery is effective as it exceeds the bounds of the domestic sphere, but it also functions in more particular ways. The "heath" ALLUDES to the setting of Emily Brontë's *Wuthering Heights*, while the "tree / Their brush" recalls Emily Carr, who painted the majestic forests of British Columbia's West Coast. The most striking INTERTEXTUAL element here lies in that "wandering lonely" of line II. Those words might be familiar to you; they echo the Romantic poet William Wordsworth's well-known poem, "I Wandered Lonely as a Cloud." In that poem, the speaker witnesses the stunning natural scene of an endless trail of waving daffodils, a vision which returns to him afterwards. The poem resonates with the concerns of Livesay's exploration; not only does Wordsworth's speaker witness the daffodils thanks to a solitary walk, but the scene is later summoned by the "inward eye / Which is the bliss of solitude" (21–22). Wordsworth famously defined poetry as "the spontaneous overflow of powerful feelings: it takes its origin from emotion recollected in tranquility" (Preface 21). The three Emilys, unlike Livesay's speaker, were afforded the "tranquility" necessary to recollect, reflect, and compose.

Stanza three returns to the image of crying Emilys, from whom the speaker hears "reproach." What does she imagine they are reproachful about? Do they envy her family life? Do they criticize her for sacrificing her artistic career? The following lines describe "their inner storm / Of separate man in woman's form," articulating the difficulty women have faced balancing creative ambitions and social expectations. That a writer or artist would be figured as "separate man" reinforces the idea that achievement is dependent on a certain amount of autonomy, and underlines too the gendering of our traditional models of creativity. The speaker then names the "kingdom, barred / To them," marriage and motherhood, figuring these as natural drives flowing through her "arteries"; does she view these as intrinsic to "woman's form"? Do the Emilys weep for having had to suppress these natural drives to make space for their creativity?

The three historical Emilys would have led very different lives had they married. In nineteenth-century America, for example, a mother would have typically borne half a dozen children or more, and carried full responsibility in the domestic sphere. What's more, the Emilys lived in times when authorship for women was deemed at the same time inappropriate and beyond their intellectual capabilities. Emily Brontë and her sisters published under male pseudonyms because "authoresses are liable to be looked on with prejudice" (C. Brontë ix-xvi). Canadian Emily Carr was not considered a person under the law until she was almost sixty. But Dorothy Livesay was born in the twentieth century. Why is she "born to hear" the conflicted cries of her foremothers? Well, while times have started to change, with men sharing more of the domestic labour and women's achievements gaining recognition, let's look at the year of Livesay's poem: 1953. The 1950s were a particularly hostile decade for women with ambitions outside the home. During World War II, women took on all manner of jobs to replace the men who had gone into military service. But following the war, there was a massive cultural movement to evacuate women from the paid workforce and encourage them to resume their prewar roles as unpaid domestic labourers. This would not have been an encouraging environment for a woman who wished to balance family life and career.

Research tip: A subject encyclopedia would be an excellent source of historical information about the social climate of this era. Another way to get a feel for the milieu Livesay wrote in is to look at popular magazines from that time. Issues of the widely circulated *LIFE* magazine are a click away through Google Books. Check out the advertisements in a few of the issues from the 1950s. (You might remember, too, that this was the atmosphere in which Sylvia Plath was writing.) What models of womanhood are presented? Have you ever seen so many women in bridal gowns? You'll also find a writer in an ad: Ernest Hemingway selling Ballantine beer, so refreshing "when you have worked a big marlin fast because there were sharks after him" (57). Looking at the cultural images your subject would have been looking at can give you unique insight into the social pressures of their environment.

Livesay's speaker faces, along with other female authors, the competing pulls of domestic life and writing life. The swing in the poem between images of crying Emilys and images of free and powerful Emilys reflects this tension in the psyche of our speaker. We can see the conflict most succinctly and powerfully conveyed if we return to lines 19–20:

I yet possess another kingdom, barred
To them, these three, this Emily.

Here Livesay deploys ENJAMBMENT in order to crystallize the tension addressed in her poem. Read as a sentence, the meaning is clear: the speaker chose a life (of marriage and motherhood) that the others did not. But LINEATION is a meaningful feature of poetry; cutting the line after "barred" allows for another reading of that line. Grammar is momentarily suspended and we read that the speaker's domestic kingdom is "barred"; in other words, she likens marriage to a prison. The stanza's conclusion confirms this reading, as the speaker laments enjoying creative liberty "only for a brief span."

Also interesting in line 20 is the transformation of the three Emilys into "this Emily." The literary foremothers are represented together as a monolithic figure. The speaker herself gets to be "an Emily" when afforded time to devote to her work. If we read Emily as embodying artistic drive, then that could be what is crying "to be set free—" within the mind of the speaker in stanza one. The dash there allows for some undecidability, for multiple readings, while serving as a nod to Emily Dickinson's similarly complicating practice of using dashes.

The poem appears to end in a reversal of the first stanza, with the complaining Emilys now "triumphant." PARADOXICALLY, the speaker's "whole" (akin to today's notion of "having it all": family and career) does not measure up. Echoing the word from line 2, now she is the "one / Uncomforted." Still, the last word does not rest. Livesay has placed a colon at the end of line 30, which ambiguates the conclusion, allowing for "I am the one / Uncomforted" to be spoken by the monolithic Emily. The complexity of identity and identification here further dramatizes the connections between the modern writer and her foremothers: the power of Brontë, Dickinson, Carr "And others whom I will not name" to inspire women authors who came after them, their shared experience of vexed life choices, their ambition in the face of worlds slow to embrace women as serious writers.

More Feminist Poems

Some questions to get you started:

"Prologue": What strategies does Bradstreet use to get away with writing poetry in seventeenth-century Puritan New England? Do stanzas five and six colour your reading of the other stanzas? "In an Artist's Studio": How does Rossetti complicate the way we think about the figure of Muse? "Sheltered Garden": How does H.D. use the image of a garden to reveal the oppressive nature of a notion popular in her time, that women must be sheltered and protected? "Blues Spiritual for Mammy Prater": How and why does Brand turn the passive experience of posing for a photograph into an action replete with intention? "Body Politics": The speaker of this poem relates what "Mama said" about womanhood, particularly aboriginal womanhood; do you imagine the speaker as among the "Real women," the "city women," or somewhere in between?

Prologue

To sing of Wars, of Captains, and of Kings,
Of Cities founded, Common-wealths begun,
For my mean° Pen are too superior things;   *lowly*
Or how they all, or each their dates have run,
5 Let Poets and Historians set these forth.
My obscure lines shall not so dim their worth.

But when my wond'ring eyes and envious heart
Great Bartas'° sugar'd lines do but read o'er,   *16th-century French writer*
Fool, I do grudge the Muses did not part
10 'Twixt him and me that over-fluent store.
A Bartas can do what a Bartas will

But simple I according to my skill.

From School-boy's tongue no Rhet'ric we expect,
Nor yet a sweet Consort° from broken strings,   *harmony*
15 Nor perfect beauty where's a main defect.
My foolish, broken, blemished Muse so sings,
And this to mend, alas, no Art is able,
'Cause Nature made it so irreparable.

Nor can I, like that fluent sweet-tongued Greek°   *Demosthenes*
20 Who lisp'd at first, in future times speak plain.
By Art he gladly found what he did seek,
A full requital of his striving pain.
Art can do much, but this maxim's most sure:
A weak or wounded brain admits no cure.

25 I am obnoxious to each carping tongue
Who says my hand a needle better fits.
A Poet's Pen all scorn I should thus wrong,
For such despite they cast on female wits.
If what I do prove well, it won't advance,
30 They'll say it's stol'n, or else it was by chance.

But sure the antique Greeks were far more mild,
Else of our Sex, why feigned they those nine°   *muses of arts and sciences*
And poesy made Calliope's° own child?   *muse of epic poetry*
So 'mongst the rest they placed the Arts divine,
35 But this weak knot they will full soon untie.
The Greeks did nought but play the fools and lie.

Let Greeks be Greeks, and Women what they are.
Men have precedency and still excel;
It is but vain unjustly to wage war.
40 Men can do best, and Women know it well.
Preeminence in all and each is yours;
Yet grant some small acknowledgement of ours.

And oh ye high flown quills that soar the skies,
And ever with your prey still catch your praise,
45 If e'er you deign these lowly lines your eyes,
Give thyme or Parsley wreath, I ask no Bays.[1]
This mean and unrefined ore of mine
Will make your glist'ring gold but more to shine.

—Anne Bradstreet, 1650

In an Artist's Studio

One face looks out from all his canvases,
One selfsame figure sits or walks or leans:
We found her hidden just behind those screens,
That mirror gave back all her loveliness.
5 A queen in opal or in ruby dress,
A nameless girl in freshest summer-greens,
A saint, an angel—every canvas means
The same one meaning, neither more nor less.
He feeds upon her face by day and night,
10 And she with true kind eyes looks back on him,
Fair as the moon and joyful as the light:
Not wan with waiting, not with sorrow dim;
Not as she is, but was when hope shone bright;
Not as she is, but as she fills his dream.

—Christina Rossetti, 1896

Sheltered Garden

I have had enough.
I gasp for breath.

Every way ends, every road,
every foot-path leads at last
5 to the hill-crest—
then you retrace your steps,

---

1   *Bays*: Poet's crown made with bay laurel.

or find the same slope on the other side,
precipitate.°   *steep*

I have had enough—
10 border-pinks, clove-pinks, wax-lilies,
herbs, sweet-cress.

O for some sharp swish of a branch—
there is no scent of resin
in this place,
15 no taste of bark, of coarse weeds,
aromatic, astringent—
only border on border of scented pinks.

Have you seen fruit under cover
that wanted light—
20 pears wadded in cloth,
protected from the frost,
melons, almost ripe,
smothered in straw?

Why not let the pears cling
25 to the empty branch?
All your coaxing will only make
a bitter fruit—
let them cling, ripen of themselves,
test their own worth,
30 nipped, shrivelled by the frost,
to fall at last but fair
with a russet coat.

Or the melon—
let it bleach yellow
35 in the winter light,
even tart to the taste—
it is better to taste of frost—

the exquisite frost—
than of wadding and of dead grass.

40   For this beauty,
beauty without strength,
chokes out life.
I want wind to break,
scatter these pink-stalks,
45   snap off their spiced heads,
fling them about with dead leaves—
spread the paths with twigs,
limbs broken off,
trail great pine branches,
50   hurled from some far wood
right across the melon-patch,
break pear and quince—
leave half-trees, torn, twisted
but showing the fight was valiant.

55   O to blot out this garden
to forget, to find a new beauty
in some terrible
wind-tortured place.

                    —H.D. (Hilda Doolittle), 1916

Blues Spiritual for Mammy Prater

*On looking at 'the photograph of Mammy Prater an ex-slave,
115 years old when her photograph was taken'*

she waited for her century to turn
she waited until she was one hundred and fifteen
years old to take a photograph
to take a photograph and to put those eyes in it
5   she waited until the technique of photography was
suitably developed
to make sure the picture would be clear

to make sure no crude daguerreotype would lose
her image
10 would lose her lines and most of all her eyes
and her hands
she knew the patience of one hundred and fifteen years
she knew that if she had the patience,
to avoid killing a white man
15 that I would see this photograph
she waited until it suited her
to take this photograph and to put those eyes in it.

in the hundred and fifteen years which it took her to
wait for this photograph she perfected this pose
20 she sculpted it over a shoulder of pain,
a thing like despair which she never called
this name for she would not have lasted
the fields, the ones she ploughed
on the days that she was a mule, left
25 their etching on the gait of her legs
deliberately and unintentionally
she waited, not always silently, not always patiently,
for this self portrait
by the time she sat in her black dress, white collar,
30 white handkerchief, her feet had turned to marble,
her heart burnished red,
and her eyes.

she waited one hundred and fifteen years
until the science of photography passed tin and
35 talbotype for a surface sensitive enough
to hold her eyes
she took care not to lose the signs
to write in those eyes what her fingers could not script
a pact of blood across a century, a decade and more
40 she knew then that it would be me who would find
her will, her meticulous account, her eyes,
her days when waiting for this photograph

was all that kept her sane
she planned it down to the day,
45 the light,
the superfluous photographer
her breasts,
her hands
this moment of
50 my turning the leaves of a book,
noticing, her eyes.

                      —Dionne Brand, 1990

Body Politics

Mama said,

Real women
don't steal
from the sky and wear clouds
5 on their eyelids.

Real women
eat rabbit well-done
not left half-raw
on their mouth.

10 Real women
have lots of meat
on their bones.
They're not starving,
hobbled horses
15 with bony, grinding hips.

Real women caress
with featherstone hands
not with falcon fingernails
that have never worked.

20 When she was finished talking
    she clicked her teeth
    lifted her arse
    and farted
    at the passing
25 city women.

                    —Louise Bernice Halfe, 1994

A Brief Guide to Meter

YOUR HEARTBEAT, YOUR FOOTSTEPS, the in and out of your breath: these are the measure of your being in the world. No wonder we respond so viscerally to the rhythmic patterns of poetry—we're regular walking poems! Meter, the underlying beat structure of a poem, contributes to the musicality that makes poetry pleasurable. Before poetry was written down, meter also served as a mnemonic device; like rhyme, meter supplied patterns that facilitated memorization.

Most of the poetry written in the twentieth and twenty-first centuries diverges from the regular meters we see in the traditional CANON. I'll talk about the dominant form of contemporary poetry, FREE VERSE, at the end of this chapter. Understanding how free verse functions will be easier once we have a sense of the tradition of poetic meters.

Most people have heard of IAMBIC PENTAMETER. This meter features ten-syllable lines comprised of five feet, each FOOT made up of an unstressed and a stressed syllable. Iambic pentameter is one of many possible patterns in a system of meter that attends to stress (or accent) and syllable counts. This is the system we'll talk about here, but you should know that it's not the only system. Before the Renaissance, poets focused on the number of accented syllables in a line, but were less concerned about the number of unaccented syllables. In Classical literature, attention was paid to the length of syllables, rather than to accent. Another system highlights syllable count only. We will stick to the ACCENTUAL-SYLLABIC system of meter because it has been the dominant system in English poetry for hundreds of years. Understanding it will equip you to identify not only iambic pentameter, the most commonly used meter of that tradition, but others as well.

Before we sharpen our ears to discern stress variations and determine syllables, let's be clear on what a syllable is. A syllable features a single vowel sound that is usually, but not always, linked to consonants. So in 'farm·hand,' for example, the two vowel sounds are each sandwiched between consonants, but in 'e·on' the first syllable consists merely of the 'e' sound. For illustration, I've inserted the dots dictionaries use to indicate syllable breaks. If you have any trouble determining the number of syllables in words, practising with a dictionary is helpful.

When we speak English, we stress certain syllables without having to think about it. Becoming conscious of those habitual stress patterns can take a little practice. SCANSION, or the analysis of metrical patterns, demands that we hone our sensitivity to the difference between accented and unaccented syllables. Start with your name. Say it aloud. Which syllable or syllables do you emphasize? One great way to figure out if you're on the right track is to try putting the stress on different syllables to see which one sounds right. Is it *Mad·i·SON*, *Mad·I·son* or *MAD·i·son*? *AN·to·ni·o*, *An·TO·ni·o*, *An·to·NI·o*, or *An·to·ni·O*? I put the stress on the first syllable of my name: *SU·san*, but the same syllables are accented differently for my friend *Su·ZANNE*.

In a line of poetry, stresses will generally fall on key words, such as verbs and nouns, while little words (*in, an, on*, etc.) are generally unstressed. Suffixes such as *-ing*, *-ment*, and *-er* are also unstressed. You'll find that syllables which take longer to articulate often demand more stress than short syllables; although *through* and *to* are both prepositions, the former is more likely to be stressed. Rhetorical emphasis can also come into play. Whether you say **WILL** *you?* or *will* **YOU?** depends on the context. As you can imagine, determining rhetorical stress like this is subject to reader interpretation. In truth, all scansion is to some degree subjective. Different readers will scan the same line in slightly different ways. So don't fret about discerning a single "right" scansion; just bring all you've learned about the practice to your analysis and do what seems most accurate to you.

To scan a line, we mark the stressed and unstressed syllables. (This is another aspect of the process complicated by divergent methods: the markings, and range of markings, will vary among critics. I'm introducing you to the system you'll encounter most often.) Mark stressed syllables with an **ictus** (´) and unstressed syllables with a **breve** (˘). Here's an example, using a line from Anne Bradstreet's "Prologue":

˘   ´ ˘   ´ ˘   ´   ˘   ´ ˘   ´
My foolish, broken, blemished Muse so sings,

If you try to say it with the stresses placed differently, you confirm this scansion. We don't say *foo•LISH* or *bro•KEN*.

Now figure out which pattern of stress gets repeated. In this case it's the pattern: unstressed syllable + stressed syllable (˘ ´). This repeated unit is a foot, and this particular pattern comprises an IAMB, or IAMBIC FOOT. Can you think of some words or combinations of words that make up an iamb? Here are a few examples: *balLOON, deCEIVE, of COURSE*. The iambic foot is the most common in poetry written in English, but there are some others to know about. Here's a chart, including some words and phrases illustrating each stress pattern:

˘ ´	**iamb** (or **iambic foot**, **iambic meter**)	*helLO, reSORT,* *at LAST*
´ ˘	**trochee** (**trochaic**)	*SWIMming, WRITE to, BANner*
˘ ˘ ´	**anapest** (**anapestic**)	*to the PARK, interCEDE, in a DITCH*
´ ˘ ˘	**dactyl** (**dactylic**)	*MERrily, Over the, LAUGHingly*

It's important to remember that metrical feet don't necessarily align with words. The illustrative examples above include phrases that make up a foot—*in a DITCH*, for instance. But a foot can also straddle words. Look at the following iambic line from Millay's "I, Being Born a Woman and Distressed." In scansion, you delineate the feet with vertical lines:

˘   ´ | ˘ ´ | ˘   ´ | ˘   ´ | ˘ ´
For conversation when we meet again.

Note that the stress in the first foot falls on the first syllable of "conversation," and the unstressed half of the third foot falls in that word's last syllable.

There are a couple other foot types to keep in mind:

´ ´   **spondee (spondaic)**   *CARPARK, HEY YOU, ZIGZAG*
˘ ˘   **pyrrhic (pyrrhic)**   *in the, to a, the last two syllables of **MER**rily*

I've separated these off because you don't find whole poems composed in say, spondaic meter. Spondees and pyrrhics constitute momentary deviations from the standard meters (iambic, trochaic, anapestic, and dactylic) that structure a poem.

The second element to note when determining meter is the number of feet in the line. These are the terms we use:

monometer: one foot per line
dimeter: two feet per line
trimeter: three feet per line
tetrameter: four feet per line
pentameter: five feet per line
hexameter: six feet per line
heptameter: seven feet per line
octameter: eight feet per line

As an example, we can scan these famous lines by Clement Clarke Moore:

'Twas the night before Christmas, when all through the house
Not a creature was stirring, not even a mouse.

Here we find a recurring anapestic pattern, with four anapests to a line, so we say the poem is written in **anapestic tetrameter**.

Deviations, or variations, can make scansion a challenge, but they contribute to the complex musicality and expressiveness of poetry. To more easily handle the jerks and bumps of, say, an iambic poem sprinkled with the odd spondee or an anapestic meter spiked with iambs, scan the whole poem first, perhaps starting with accented syllables only. That way the dominant pattern of meter will reveal itself, so that temporary deviations can be seen for what they are. You might feel that the "Not" in the passage above should be stressed, or at least fall somewhere between stressed and unstressed; this distinction of intermediate stress is commonly marked with an accent **grave**: ˋ . But scanning the whole poem reveals that moment as an enriching variation, rather than bespeaking the metrical backbone, which is anapestic tetrameter.

Once you get scanning, you'll start to notice certain variations cropping up again and again. One you'll see a lot is a trochee occupying the foot (frequently the first) of an iambic pentameter line, a move we call **trochaic substitution**. Here are the first two lines of Claude McKay's "The Castaways," scanned. Read them aloud:

The vivid grass with visible delight

Springing triumphant from the pregnant earth;

You'll hear that in the second line, the first foot is a trochee rather than an iamb. As always when we note a surprising poetic event, we ask "Why? How does this trochaic substitution contribute to meaning?" This one's pretty clear: the enthusiasm of that springing grass is emphasized by a gung-ho stress that couldn't wait for the second syllable to appear! (Note also my use of the accent grave on the last syllable of "visible"; here it's deployed for its other use, as a marker for the expected stress of the iamb. While, because of its placement in a line of iambic pentameter, we give "-ble" more emphasis than we would if we encountered the word "visible" in prose, reading it as a full stress would sound unnatural.)

Another common variation is **spondaic substitution**. Here's the second quatrain from Shakespeare's Sonnet 73, scanned:

In me thou see'st the twilight of such day

As after sunset fadeth in the west,

Which by and by black night doth take away,

／　　　／|◡　　◡　／　|◡　　　／|◡　／|◡　／
Death's second self, that seals up all in rest.

In this case, that fourth line begins with a double whammy: two stresses in place of the iamb. This first foot really stands out, emphasizing the spectre of death, the speaker's central preoccupation. Note that "black night" in the preceding line is also a spondee, which helps underscore the parallel the speaker is drawing between the end of the day and the end of life.

Sometimes you'll find a pyrrhic foot alongside a spondee, as in Claude McKay's "Harlem Dancer":

◡　　／|◡　　　／　|◡　／　|◡　／　|◡　／
To me she seemed a proudly-swaying palm
　／　　　／|◡◡|◡　／　|◡　　　／　|◡　／
Grown lovelier for passing through a storm.

The initial spondee of the second line there lends emphasis to the counterintuitive (in conventional poetry, at least) notion that hardship can make a woman more beautiful. The pyrrhic following renders the spondee all the more forceful, throwing it into relief. And despite this effective metrical deviation, the combination of spondee and pyrrhic ensures a satisfying balance of stressed and unstressed syllables in the line.

Often you will come across lines featuring an extra syllable. Frequently these syllables are unaccented and appear at the end of a line; in this case we don't regard them as foot substitutions, but rather an acceptable variation on the final foot (occasionally you see this before a CAESURA too). To scan this extra syllable, traditionally termed a FEMININE ENDING—as opposed to the MASCULINE (stressed-syllable) ENDING—place the breve in parentheses as I do here in Shakespeare's Sonnet 20:

◡　　／|◡　／|◡　　　／　|◡　／　|◡　／(◡)
And for a woman wert thou first created,
◡　／|◡　＼|◡　　　／　|◡　／|◡　／(◡)
Till Nature as she wrought thee fell a-doting,

‿ ╱|‿╱|‿ ╱|‿ ╱|‿ ╱ (‿)
And by addition me of thee defeated,

‿ ╱|‿ ╱| ╱ ‿|‿ ╱|‿ ╱ (‿)
By adding one thing to my purpose nothing.

While I applaud the move to change the term **feminine ending** to the now popular **extra-syllable ending** or **hypermetrical ending**, knowing the traditional sexist terminology contributes to the humour of this sonnet. The extra syllable on each line wittily echoes the, ahem, "addition" Nature visited upon the speaker's beloved to render her/him physically male. That the syllabic addition to each line be termed "feminine" sustains the play with gender propelling this poem.

One common extra-syllable variation is the **anapestic substitution**, an added skip in the step of an iambic foot. Here are some examples from our text, the anapests scanned in bold:

‿ ╱| ╲   ╱|‿ ╱|‿ ╱|‿ ‿ ╱
Of my stout blood against my staggering brain,

                    (Millay, "I, Being Born")

‿ ╱|‿ ╱|‿ ‿   ╱|‿   ╱
So rested he by the Tumtum tree

                    (Carroll, "Jabberwocky")

‿ ╱|‿ ‿ ╱|‿   ╱|‿ ╲ |‿   ╱
A flowery tale more sweetly than our rhyme:

                    (Keats, "Grecian Urn")

Many anapests are essentially iambs, as one of the unstressed syllables remains unvoiced through ELISION. Millay's "staggering" could be pronounced "stag'ring," for example, and Keats's "flowery" pronounced "flow'ry." These pronunciations correspond to elisions which, in early poetry, we often see marked. Bradstreet, writing in 1650, indicates her elision of the "o" in "Rhetoric" below:

From School-boy's tongue no Rhet'ric we expect,

In lines not marked with the eliding apostrophe, readers, reciters, and actors can often make a choice about whether or not to voice an extra syllable. But as in Carroll's "by the Tumtum tree," there are plenty of anapests which can't be easily shortened through elision. The lively rhythmic variation of anapestic substitution becomes increasingly common as we move toward the Modern period.

You will also come across poems which drop a syllable. This is a frequent practice in poems featuring rhymed trochaic lines. Use the breve in parenthesis to mark the missing syllable. Here's the opening of Blake's "The Tyger":

/ ˘ | / ˘ | / ˘ | / (˘)
Tyger! Tyger! burning bright
/ ˘ | / ˘ | \ ˘ | / (˘)
In the forests of the night,

The majority of lines in the poem scan this way, so we can say the poem is written in **trochaic tetrameter catalectic**. We say the lines are CATALECTIC because they drop an expected final unaccented syllable. In the case of "The Tyger," the effect is to heighten the pounding ferocity of the poem's central image and burning question. (As a side note, see that I've used the intermediate stress mark for "of", marking its place in the trochee; although it's a small word, the relentless trochaic pattern of the poem invites a reader to stress it more than the following "the".)

There is a rhythmic peculiarity in the "The Tyger" that has inspired varying scansions. Six of the poem's twenty-four lines bear eight syllables rather than seven. Note, for example, the final lines of the first and last stanzas:

Could frame thy fearful symmetry?
. . .
Dare frame thy fearful symmetry?

These lines (along with lines 10, 11, 18, and 20) might be scanned thus: ˘ / | ˘ / | ˘ / | ˘ /. These regular iambic lines have prompted some scholars to think of "The Tyger" as a poem written in iambic tetrameter, with the variation of a dropped first syllable in most of the lines (so the meter would be termed **iambic tetrameter truncated**).

These critics would scan the first line like this:

(˘) ⁄ ˘   ⁄ ˘   ⁄ ˘   ⁄
     Tyger! Tyger! burning bright

Proponents of the trochaic tetrameter catalectic reading can scan the first syllable of the six odd lines as an extra:

(˘)   ⁄   ˘ | ⁄ ˘ | ⁄ ˘ | ⁄ (˘)
     Could frame thy fearful symmetry?

This reading makes more sense to me. When read aloud, the poem has a distinctively trochaic feel—an insistent thumping as opposed to the gentler ebb and flow characterizing iambic lines. The extra first syllables fall naturally into the gaps left by catalexis in preceding lines. What we do get is a mild emphasis on those first words, which helps to underscore the shift from "Could" in the first stanza to "Dare" in the last, as the speaker's awe escalates. We are walking poems, not robots; debates about how to scan meter testify to both the richness of poetic rhythm and the role of the individual ear in literary analysis.

If you find, when scanning a poem, that there are a confusing number of foot variations, yet a consistency in the number of stresses per line, you might be dealing with ACCENTUAL VERSE. The accentual-syllabic system we've been discussing took hold in English poetry during the Elizabethan period. Before that, poetry in English was composed without strict attention to the number of unaccented syllables per line. Although accentual-syllabic verse dominated literary practice from the Renaissance until the Modern period, accentual meter persisted in popular oral forms. This looser mode began to regain popularity during the nineteenth century, so we see it in the Modern and contemporary contexts as well. You can probably discover many examples of accentual meter within your own memorized repertoire of children's nursery rhymes, such as:

⁄ ˘ ˘   ⁄ ˘ ˘   ⁄ ˘   ⁄
Pat-a-cake, pat-a-cake, baker's man,

/ ˘ ˘ / ˘ / ˘ ˘ /
Bake me a cake, as fast as you can;

/ ˘ / ˘ ˘ / ˘ ˘ ˘/
Pat it, roll it, and mark it with a B,

˘ / ˘ ˘ ˘ / ˘ ˘ / ˘ ˘ ˘ /
And put it in the oven for baby and me.

I've included the breves in my scansion just to illustrate that they form no consistent pattern. It's really the four accents per line that constitute the pulse of the poem.

If you scan a poem and find consistency in neither syllable count nor accent, you've landed in the realm of free verse, the most common form of poetry written in English today. As the twentieth century neared, poets began experimenting with a more flexible approach to meter. While debate on the value of free verse was fierce—Robert Frost famously declared that writing free verse is like playing tennis without a net—the form rapidly gained popularity among poets eager to expand the possibilities of the poetic line. Ezra Pound offered a useful articulation of the free verse poet's ambition: "to compose in the sequence of the musical phrase, not in sequence of a metronome" (36). Free verse bears neither regular meter nor regular rhyme. So does this mean your newly acquired expertise in scansion is irrelevant to Modern and contemporary poetry? Not at all! It's just that you'll be thinking about stress in different ways. Rather than identifying an underlying meter and the subtle ways a poem deviates from that traditional pattern, you'll be finding a rhythmic profile unique to a given poem. You're likely to spot moments that fall into an original pattern, or rhythmic occurrences that contribute to meaning. Here's the short poem by Ezra Pound you encountered in Chapter 9:

˘ ˘ / ˘ ˘ ˘ / ˘
In a Station of the Metro

˘ ˘ ˘ / ˘ ˘ ˘ / ˘ ˘ ˘ /
The apparition of these faces in the crowd;

/ ˘ ˘ ˘ / / /
Petals on a wet, black bough.

No familiar meter announces itself here, so we can call this free verse. But the arrangement of stressed and unstressed syllables is still highly relevant to a discussion of this poem. We can see that, including the title, the poem proceeds with a ratio of three unstressed syllables for every stress, up until we get to the three accents of "wet, black bough." The effect is to invite a slow, pronounced reading of the poem's conclusion; the reader tends to dwell on each of the last three words for the duration it took to enunciate four syllables a line earlier. This rhythmic event contributes to meaning. First, the emphasis foregrounds the striking final image. Secondly, it compels us to slow our consumption of it to the extent that we enter the kind of meditative state most conducive to appreciating the equation of scenes proposed.

Consider the stress-heavy rhythm of Gwendolyn Brooks's "We Real Cool":

We Real Cool

THE POOL PLAYERS.
SEVEN AT THE GOLDEN SHOVEL.

We real cool. We
Left school. We

Lurk late. We
Strike straight. We

Sing sin. We
Thin gin. We

Jazz June. We
Die soon.

Here again, scanning the lines reveals no traditional meter, yet a unique pattern governs the form. Eight three-syllable sentences are staggered so that "We" appears at the end of all but the last line. One could argue that every syllable of the poem is accented, helping to convey the energy and bravado of the speakers. If any syllable of the lines is unstressed, or of intermediate stress, it's the final "We," a less remarkable word than the others. Yet its repetition all down the right border of the poem serves to foreground it. The uncertain status of that pronoun, heightened by its terminal position in the line, which leaves the subject floating, communicates the fraught existence of these young men. They are at once formidable and vulnerable.

Developing scansion skills provides you with an important tool in your exploration of how poems mean. Knowing about meter enables you to identify, for example, fourteen iambic pentameter lines as a SONNET or QUATRAINS of alternating tetrameter and trimeter lines as a BALLAD. Being able to place a poem within the tradition of these established stanza forms enables you to consider how that poem chimes with or challenges its traditional context. You will also be able, in both fixed forms and free verse, to articulate the ways patterns of stress contribute to the effect of poetic language. Whether a text conveys a tone of playfulness, fury, solemnity, urgency, anxiety, or peace, chances are you can find in its rhythms the signature of that tone.

How to Write about Poetry

A FEW TIMES IN THIS book I've introduced the idea of you entering a conversation about poetry. This conversation can be informal and intimate, a dialogue within a group of friends or a class; but it can also be more far-reaching, engaging a body of published criticism. In developing your skills as a composer of essays about poetry, you can begin to share your unique perspective with not only your peers and instructors, but the greater world of readers and critics, too. Writing an essay well is key to communicating your position and enriching the field of discussion around a given work. And, let's be honest, if you're reading this book you're also thinking about a short-term goal: getting a good grade on your paper.

With this last point in mind, let me qualify this chapter. I am going to guide you through the planning and composing of a student essay, offering advice on topics, research, structure, diction, etc. But you've also got to pay close attention to the parameters of the assignment your instructor has given you. They may ask that you do no outside research, or that your essay be written in a specific format, or that your discussion address historical context. To earn that grade, you should also note their pet peeves and preferences. A professor might ask you not to use the first person ("I"), or to avoid long quotations, or to assume the tone of a formal argument. In short, I'm offering you a general guide, but be sure to remain flexible so you can adapt to given assignments.

In order to explore the composition of an essay, I'll take you through one student's writing experience. Jacob was given the assignment to write an essay of 1000-1500 words on the poem "Aunt Jennifer's Tigers," by Adrienne Rich. He was asked to include a Works

Cited page comprised of at least three entries, indicating that some secondary research should be considered.

When Jacob first read "Aunt Jennifer's Tigers," Rich's portrait of a woman in an oppressive marriage, he kept thinking about William Blake's poem, "The Tyger." For a moment he thought he was just getting his poems mixed up, and returned his focus to the specifics of the Rich poem—the rhyme scheme, the figurative language, the images. He scribbled all over his copy of the poem, a great way to actively examine the work and start making connections. In pursuing these details, however, Jacob realized the links to the Blake poem were formal as well as thematic. The rhymed quatrain format was the same, for example, and line 2 of each poem mentions a setting. He realized he may have landed on a topic, his original contribution to discussion of this poem. The Blake ALLUSION flagged a dynamic of INTERTEXTUALITY. But identifying intertextual connections would not make for a meaty enough thesis. In order to come up with a thesis, he needed to push a little further, think about how that intertextuality inflected the meaning of the poem. After meditating on it a bit, Jacob came up with a bold idea: If Blake was asking who could have created this awesome beast, Rich had a surprising answer: Aunt Jennifer. This possibility spurred Jacob to look again at the two poems, and he found even more points of connection between them that further supported his conclusion.

Scribbling all over a copy of the poem is a tried and true method of recording insights and making connections (see facing page).

After working excitedly on his own analysis, Jacob sought out published criticism on the poem. Doing secondary research is always an adventure. There's a bit of trial and error, and investigation can follow multiple paths. Jacob knew to be wary of non-authoritative online sources such as personal blogs and student discussion forums. He began with the catalogue of his university library, and immediately located the original collection in which "Aunt Jennifer's Tigers" appeared, finding there Auden's telling introduction to the volume, which turned out to be important to his analysis. Aside from this library search, Jacob found three resources particularly helpful. He used the *MLA International Bibliography*, inputting search terms such as "Aunt Jennifer's Tigers" and "Adrienne Rich" and "Blake." He

Connection to Blake

A to his Q?

Aunt Jennifer's (Tigers)

Blake: Tyger, Tyger
Burning Bright

— *Embroidery*

a   Aunt Jennifer's tigers prance across a screen,

a   Bright topaz denizens of a world of green. —— *Line 2 of Blake*
    also about habita

b   They do not fear the men beneath the tree;

b   They pace in sleek chivalric certainty.

Ref to lamb?

a   Aunt Jennifer's fingers fluttering through her wool

a   Find even the ivory needle hard to pull. *Is this Blake's hammer?*

    hyperbole
b   The massive weight of Uncle's wedding band

b   Sits heavily upon Aunt Jennifer's hand.

Is this the "dread clasp":

a   When Aunt is dead, her terrified hands will lie

a   Still ringed with ordeals she was mastered by.

b   The tigers in the panel that she made   *Theme of*
                                              immortality
b   Will go on prancing, proud and unafraid *through ART*

Adrienne Rich, (1951)

Post WWII period of
cultural pressure on women

ALLITERATION - SOFT/HARD SOUNDS

also searched under Google Books using these terms. Google Books showed him very brief excerpts featuring these terms, taken from a variety of books. From this information he could determine which books he'd like to look at. The third resource is less obvious, but it's one every experienced critic knows about: the Works Cited lists from the articles and books you've found. Jacob noticed that many articles on Rich cited her essay, "When We Dead Awaken: Writing as Revision," which appears in her collection *On Lies, Secrets, and Silence: Selected Prose 1966-1978*. Recurring references to this essay pointed to its status as a touchstone in the critical conversation about Rich, prompting Jacob to seek it out. The first article he found through the MLA database was interesting, but he did not end up engaging it directly in his paper; it was the Works Cited of that first article that opened up productive paths of research for Jacob, leading him to two books he did end up quoting in his essay. A plain old Google search can also yield possibilities. The first link appearing when Jacob Googled "Adrienne Rich Blake" took him to the website of publisher W.W. Norton and the blurb Nadine Gordimer wrote on the back of one of Rich's books: "Adrienne Rich is the Blake of American Letters." He jotted down that little gem, knowing it would resonate with his analysis.

In the course of his investigations, Jacob discovered that others mention the connection to Blake in "Aunt Jennifer's Tigers." He was somewhat disappointed that his observation had not been an original one, and wondered if he should abandon the idea. This is a common experience! Don't be discouraged if your 'original' idea turns out not to be as original as you thought. Instead, take this as a sign that you are developing the reading skills of professional, published critics. And, more importantly, know that your position will indeed be unique within the more focussed topic you've arrived at. When you discover that another critic has come up with the same finding, don't throw his or her article up in the air in despair; read it with a fine-toothed comb. What you'll discover is that you can now enter into the critical dialogue at a very specific, sophisticated level, and really make some waves. Jacob found critics pointing to the intertextuality, in statements such as this:

> The tigers' aesthetic energy, taking on a symbolic dimension and energy from William Blake's "Tyger," contrasts sharply with Aunt Jennifer's inner fears, her outer silence, and submissiveness. (Langdell 26)

While a few critics noted this contrast, the formidable tigers really throwing into relief the meekness of Aunt Jennifer, nobody went so far as Jacob had in thinking that Rich is giving Blake a response to his question. Neither did the critics he found articulate links between the poems beyond there being tigers in them. Jacob could explicate the intertextual resonances he found in support of his thesis that Rich's poem serves as an answer to Blake's.

Now Jacob was ready to plan his essay. He had his scribbled-up poem and some notes he'd taken from secondary research. I find the best thing to do when preparing for writing is get working on another scribbly page. That is, start writing down all your points, your thoughts, your questions, your agreements and disagreements with critics. Not all that you note down will end up in your essay, but at this stage just include everything. You'll find that points start to coalesce into groups, and this is how you can begin imagining your paragraphs, and the order in which you'd like to deliver stages of your argument.

I say "argument" because many critical essays are composed around a central thesis, which you prove with evidence from the text. Jacob's essay turned out to be an argument. But a critical essay can also proceed as an exploration, or as a raising of new issues, or as a mystery to be solved. The go-to format for high school essays is often the five-paragraph essay: an introductory paragraph (which starts in general terms and narrows down to your thesis), three proof paragraphs, and a concluding paragraph (which restates the thesis and then broadens out at the end). Although this may feel formulaic now, there's actually nothing wrong with the five-paragraph essay if that organization suits your discussion. The key to successful essay form is to let the specificity of what you want to say determine the shape of delivery. Jacob, for example, worried it was weird to delay his thesis until the end of the second paragraph; but it was more logical to address a number of points before arriving at that thesis, so he wisely let the internal logic of his argument govern the shape. Like a poem, an essay is creative work. It is your original piece of writing, and it's up to you to compose and orchestrate it for maximal effect.

With a map for his essay in hand, Jacob began composing. Some insights arose in the process of writing, a common—and rewarding—experience. The creative work of composition tends to spark new ideas. As you write each sentence, consider the most lucid and elegant way of expressing your point. When an idea or a phrasing feels a bit fuzzy or muddled, ask yourself the question, "What am I really trying to say here?" Along the way, you might revise some points, or even reorganize your original outline.

Jacob's assignment allowed for initial and revised submissions. Usually you don't get this second chance, so it's a good idea to give yourself lead time so that a friend (or you, after sleeping on it) can give the draft a fresh look. What follows is the first draft of Jacob's paper, with instructor's edits.

Class, Prof, date?

Name, page

Jacob Young

"Aunt Jennifer's Tigers"   *title your essay*

Approach the heart of your analysis

Overly general.

Creativity is a universal drive. Many poets across
the centuries have explored this drive that shapes
innovations in every feild of human endeavour.
sp
Poet and essayist Adrian Rich was one of the most
sp!
important feminist voices in America. Critic Marianne
Whelchel states that "Rich believes in the necessity
of a feminist revolution" (52). Claire Keyes calls
Rich's poems "a threat to male supremacy" (30). Jane
Vanderbosch says that Rich "defines reality according to
a feminist aesthetic" (112). "Aunt Jennifer's Tigers,"

Rich's feminism a well-established fact — don't need evidence

might want to cite date
one of her early poems, offered a critique of marriage
vt
in a patriarchal society. The poem portrayed a woman
vt
who bears "the massive weight of Uncle's wedding band"
(7). Later this image of the ring is recalled when she
is described as a woman "ringed with ordeals she was
mastered by" (10). The ring, or "wedding band," is a
noun that Rich cleverly repeats as a verb, "ringed," so
cliché
its clear where the trials and tribulations are coming

overexplained — can you be more concise?

use present tense when discussing text

from. As unlike Aunt Jennifer as possible are the proud
and brave tigers she has embroidered. This lends the
ref
poem energy. Several critics have suggested that the
tigers are an allusion to the beast in Blake's famous
poem "The Tyger." "The tigers' aesthetic energy, taking   *IQ*
on a symbolic dimension and energy from William Blake's
"Tyger," contrasts sharply with Aunt Jennifer's inner

fears, her outer silence, and submissiveness" (Langdell 26). I suggest that the inter textual connection between these two marvelous works is even more profound, and therefore the feminist message more radical.

avoid evaluative statements - this is not a review

In both overt and subtle ways, the poet makes the [ww] difference between the tigers and Aunt Jennifer. The tigers are "unafraid" (12) and, more specificly, they [sp] "do not fear the men" (3), whereas as Aunt Jennifer has "terrified hands" (9). The two most prominent (instances) of alliteration in the poem (serves) to differentiate [s/v] the figures. The tigers are "prancing, proud" (12). Aunt Jennifer possesses "fingers fluttering" (5).

I like this illustration but can you also determine phonetic terms for these sounds?

These consonant sounds convey a distinct difference in character, in energy; the former recalls a popping balloon, while the latter sounds more like a balloon's slow deflation. Rich's difference [ww] of figures in the poem is aided in no small part by the spectre of Blake's canonical tigers, however Blake's poem is more than [AH!] a striking portrait. It is also a variously repeated urgent question, "What immortal hand or eye / Dare frame thy fearful symmetry?" Blake wants to know who could [:] [—Blake or his speaker?] have created such an awe-inspiring beast. I think it's [line #s] possible that Adrian Rich's poem furnishes that question

State more forcefully — this is your argument!

with an answer: Aunt Jennifer.

vt (for extratextual history, use past tense)

"The Tyger" occupies a special place in the

Can you cite some proof?

imagination of Adrian Rich. It is not surprising that Blake that should supply the image electrifying Rich's poem and that, further, "Aunt Jennifer's Tigers" might be seen as a response to his question. The formal [awk] equivalencies in the two poems show Rich is answering

Blake. Both poems have <u>four-line stanzas</u>. Both poems
are comprised of rhyming couplets. The second line of
[*quatrains*]
Blake's poem states the tigers' habitat "in the forests
of the night;" Rich follows suit, her second line
celebrating the "Bright topaz denizens of a world of
green." Note in that line the word "Bright," recalling
Blake's famous <u>opening</u>. Other points of resonance
[*quote it!* ¶]
between the poems point more specifically to my thesis
[*awk rep*]
that Rich's poem supplies a response to Blake's burning
[*quote it!*]
question. "The Tyger" is really consumed with the
creator of the beast rather than the beast itself. The
word "hand" appears four times in the poem. The speaker
[*use " " and indicate line #s*]
wonders "what dread grasp" (15) could <u>frame, seize and
clasp</u> in the creation of the fearsome tiger. In Rich's
poem we see corresponding references to "Aunt Jennifer's
hand" (8), "her terrified hands" (9) and those "fingers
fluttering." Blake's speaker muses about this creator's
tools; imagining a "hammer," a "chain" (13) and an
[*;*]
"anvil" (15). Rich puts these speculations to rest
with a surprising answer; the tigers were made with an
[*space*]
"ivory needle" (6). To Blake's incredulous question,
"Did he who made the Lamb make thee?" (20), Rich's poem
responds in the affirmative, a 'yes' subtly suggested
in the "wool" (5) Aunt Jennifer is using. While most
critics focus on the contrast between Aunt Jennifer and
her embroidered tigers, close investigation of the poem
alongside its Blakean intertext reveals another
axis fruitful of comparison, that between Blake's
imagined creator and Rich's unassuming Aunt Jennifer.
To the question of what an artist, a writer, a creator

looks like Rich presents Aunt Jennifer. *Can you discuss a little further the feminist message here?*

On the back cover of Rich's 1995 collection, Dark

ital Fields of the Republic, Nadine Gordimer declared,

save this great quotation for the end? "Adrienne Rich is the Blake of American Letters."

Just as "The Tyger" can be read in part as Blake's interrogation of his own creative power, "Aunt Jennifer's Tigers" engages Rich's fraught position as a writer. In her 1971 essay, "When we Dead Awaken: Writing as Revision," Rich recalls writing the poem back in the *colloq* day:

Quotations of 4 lines or less can be incorporated into your paragraph

"I thought I was creating a portrait of an imaginary woman. But this woman suffers from the opposition of her imagination, worked out in tapestry, and her life-style, 'ringed with ordeals she was mastered by'." (40)

Later in life it is clear to her that this figure was a *r/o* refraction of Rich herself, Rich was a young woman torn ∧ between artistic ambition and societal expectations. The poem appeared in her first collection, ∧auspiciously *title?* introduced by W.H. Auden. But his introduction bears the stamp of the chauvenism of his era. Auden praises the *sp* book: "…the poems a reader will encounter in this book are neatly and modestly dressed, speak quietly but do not mumble, respect their elders but are not cowed by them, and do not tell fibs…" (11). Written in the mid- *mod* 20th century, it is hard to imagine such a patronizing statement passing for praise of a male poet. To launch into the sexist cultural climate of the 1950's a poem like "Aunt Jennifer's Tigers," a poem that dares to take

on Blake in the championing of female creativity, was
a great feminist intervention. Adrian Rich intended us
to realize that a woman even like Aunt Jennifer could
possess the genius of creation. —*Do we know what Rich intended?*
page ⟩   *There's a dangling question you*
break ⟩   *might want to address here about*
                                            the role of author intention in this
                        Works Cited   *reading*

Auden, W. H. Foreword. *A Change of World*. By Adrienne
        Rich. New Haven: Yale U P, 1951. 7-11. Print.

Blake, William. "The Tyger." *The Broadview Anthology
        of Poetry*. Ed. Herbert Rosengarten and Amanda
        Goldrick-Jones. Peterborough, ON: Broadview P,
        1993. 157-58. Print.

Cooper, Jane Roberta, ed. *Reading Adrienne Rich:
Reviews and Revisions, 1951-81*. Ann Arbor: U of
Michigan P, 1984. Print.

Gordimer, Nadine. Back cover blurb for *Dark Fields
        of the Republic: Poems, 1991-1995*. By Adrienne
        Rich. New York: W. W. Norton & Company, 1995.

Keyes, Claire. "'The Angels Chiding': Snapshots of a
        Daughter-in-Law." Cooper 30-50.

Langdell, Cheri Colby. *Adrienne Rich: The Moment of
        Change*. Westport, CT: Praeger-Greenwood, 2004.
        Print.

Rich, Adrian. "Aunt Jennifer's Tigers." *A Change of
        World*. New Haven: Yale U P, 1951. 19. Print.

Rich, Adrian. Interview. The Language of Life: A
        Festival of Poets. By Bill Moyers. New York: *ital*
        Broadway Books, 1995. Print.

to indicate same author as above, use - - - -.

Rich, Adrian. "When we Dead Awaken: Writing as

Revision." <u>Lies, Secrets, and Silence: Selected</u>   *ital*

<u>Prose 1966-1978</u>. New York: W. W. Norton &

Company, 1979. 33-49. Print.

Whelchel, Marianne. "Mining the 'Earth-Deposits':

Women's History in Adrienne Rich's Poetry."

Cooper 51-71.

Vanderbosch, Jane. "Beginning Again." Cooper 111-39.

alphabetical order.

Don't be discouraged if you see lots of editorial marks and notes. Think of them as gifts, bits of advice that will help you become a better and better writer. (Writers working outside of the classroom crave this kind of input.) You may notice that as you improve over the course of your education, you don't see a decrease in professorial scribbles. While the nature of the notes changes, the response continues, a sign that instructors are interested and invested in your work.

Many professors will provide you with a key so you can decipher editorial markings. Here's my key as an example. Most of these markings are the standard ones used by teachers and editors, but I have (as most educators do) some pet peeves, and for these there are idiosyncratic symbols. My students know, for example, when they see AH!, that they have committed the error of using "however" as a conjunction. I know someone who uses a rubber stamp bearing an angry devil to signal a cliché. His students are very careful to express themselves in a thoughtful and original manner. Whatever it takes!

Dr. Susan Holbrook
Key to Editorial Markings

sp   spelling error

awk   awkward phrasing

∧   insert something (e.g.: ∧ ∧)
　　　　　　　　　　　　the　;

awk rep   awkward repetition

ww   wrong word

IQ   incorporate quotation into your paragraph grammatically and elegantly

r/o   run-on sentence

ref   unclear referent

⌒   close up space

AH!   don't use "however" as a conjunction

s/v   problem in agreement between subject and verb

ital   use italics

vt   problem with verb tense (remember to use present tense when analyzing text)

colloq   avoid colloquial language

frag   sentence fragment

S;s   semicolon problem (remember the rule: Sentence; sentence.)

mod   misplaced or dangling modifier

→   indent

¶   new paragraph

∿   reverse order

℘   delete (e.g.: do not ~~cannot~~ know   proffessor)

Here are some guidelines to consider when writing and revising:

Style

Some helpful DOs and DON'Ts:

DO favour active over passive verbs for more energetic style.

DON'T summarize the poem. Imagine your reader as someone who has read the poem, but hasn't necessarily engaged with it critically.

DO vary your vocabulary. Repetition is a common writing pitfall because once you've used a word it's at the forefront of your mind, ready and willing to be deployed again. If you notice you've used the word "important" three times in a paragraph, consider some synonyms (e.g., "key").

DON'T begin and/or end with wildly general statements in an effort to satisfy the funnel-shaped introductory and concluding paragraphs of the classic five-paragraph essay.

DO aim for precision and concision. Sometimes students "pad" their sentences to fulfil a word count or to affect highfalutin diction. Either way, the result is muddy prose.

DON'T use clichés. If a turn of phrase sounds familiar, consider a fresh way of expressing its sentiment.

DO use the present tense when analyzing the poem. Although the poem was written in the past, discussion about how the poem is working is expressed in the present tense.

DON'T use colloquial language.

DO vary sentence length and syntactical structure.

DON'T evaluate the text as "masterful" or "beautiful." Your essay is not a review, but an analysis of a text already deemed worthy of study.

DO integrate quotations elegantly, rather than dropping them into your essay without grammatical logic.

Spelling and Grammar

Thanks to spell checkers, spelling errors in student essays have been greatly reduced. But don't get complacent; spell checkers don't identify correctly spelled but entirely inappropriate words! For example, they wouldn't flag the error in this sentence: "He was hair to the throne." Nor will they know that you have misspelled authors' and critics' names. I have read just as many essays about Alan Ginsburg as Allen Ginsberg. Be sure to check any spellings you aren't certain of.

Reading your paper aloud can help you identify grammar problems. If a sentence feels awkward coming out of your mouth, chances are it could use some tweaking. Here are some common grammatical errors:

1. Confusion of "It's" and "Its"

It's = It is, It has
Its = Belonging to it

E.g., It's a sonnet. The poem loses its momentum.

2. Use of "However" as a Conjunction

"However" cannot be used to join two independent clauses (two complete "sentences").

```
WRONG: It's a limerick, however it's on a serious
       topic.
 RIGHT: It's a limerick. It's on a serious topic,
       however.
```

```
WRONG: Keats died young, however he was prolific.
 RIGHT: Keats died young; however, he was prolific.
```

You should be able to remove "however" and read a complete, logical independent clause.

(You can use "however" as a modifier—e.g., "However long the poem, she'll memorize it"—but that's another story.)

3. Misuse of Semicolon

Rule: Sentence; sentence.

> WRONG: He was an enigmatic character; very mysterious
>   sometimes.
> RIGHT: He was an enigmatic character; he was very
>   mysterious sometimes.

(Note the less common function of a semicolon, deployed in place of commas to ensure clarity in a complicated list. E.g., "The poet wrote in English; French, albeit badly; German, as recalled from her youth; and Russian.")

4. Dangling Demonstrative: "This"

Don't begin a sentence with an unidentified "this" unless the referent is absolutely clear.

> WRONG: The second poem is a pastoral sonnet, featuring
>   a comic rhyming couplet at the end. This
>   compels the reader to reread the first poem in
>   the sequence.

We are not sure what "This" refers to—the pastoral mode? The fact it's a sonnet? The humour? The couplet?

> RIGHT: This humorous quality compels the reader to
>   reread the first poem in the sequence.

5. Run-On Sentences, Also Known as Comma Splices

WRONG: Blake's tiger is fearsome, the speaker is in
       awe, he wonders who could have created it.

There are three complete sentences here! You could correct the error
in a number of ways, such as:

RIGHT: Blake's speaker is in awe of the fearsome
       tiger, wondering who could have created it.
RIGHT: Blake's tiger is fearsome; the awed speaker
       wonders who could have created it.

6. Sentence Fragments

The most common sentence fragments don't look like fragments, be-
cause they're not short. Phrases can be long, however, and still not
feature the noun and verb constructions that constitute an indepen-
dent clause. Here's an example:

WRONG: In the way that poets often do, leaving out
       the final syllable in order to create a more
       emphatic line ending.

Even if you didn't know that this "sentence" is really just a string of
subordinate clauses (adverbial, gerund, and infinitive), reading it
aloud might alert you to its "unfinished" quality and prompt you to
revise. Here are a couple of possible solutions:

RIGHT: She left out the final syllable in order to
       create a more emphatic line ending, in the way
       that poets often do.
RIGHT: She truncated the line in the way that poets
       often do, leaving out the final syllable in
       order to create a more emphatic ending.

7. Dangling and Misplaced Modifiers

Dangling modifiers are words or phrases untethered to the rest of the sentence. Although your reader can usually guess what you're trying to say, they often have to overlook a nonsensical grammatical link to do so.

> **WRONG**: "Mastered by" her husband, Aunt Jennifer's embroidery represents a moment of escape.

Modifiers usually describe the subject closest to them. "Aunt Jennifer's embroidery" follows the initial modifying clause, but the embroidery is not "mastered"—Aunt Jennifer is. Revise so that the *who?* raised by the opening phrase is answered precisely.

> **RIGHT**: "Mastered by" her husband, Aunt Jennifer finds a moment of escape in her embroidery.
>
> *
>
> **WRONG**: Noting the images in the poem, untamed natural beauty is H.D.'s preference.

Who is noting the images in the poem? This sentence claims "untamed natural beauty" might be.

> **RIGHT**: Noting the images in the poem, I conclude that untamed natural beauty is H.D.'s preference.
>
> *
>
> **WRONG**: A dilemma arises for a reader familiar with Shakespeare in this stanza.

Is Shakespeare in the stanza? Is the reader in the stanza? Actually the dilemma is what's in the stanza, so the modifier "in this stanza" should be placed closer to "dilemma." A misplaced modifier differs from a dangling modifier in that the entity to be modified appears in the sentence; syntax just needs to be reorganized for clarity. In the case of the dangling modifier, the entity to be modified isn't there.

RIGHT: In this stanza, a dilemma arises for a reader familiar with Shakespeare.

Quotation and Documentation

Get your hands on the latest edition of the *MLA Handbook for Writers of Research Papers*, which details the standard methods for quotation and documentation in the Humanities. You will consult this resource throughout your academic career. There you will find answers to every citational conundrum that arises. I supply here just a quick overview of how to quote (present others' work, both primary and secondary) and cite (acknowledge sources).

Primary Sources

Quoting from your primary source (the poem) is a powerful and economical method of illustrating and propelling your analysis.

The rules for quoting poetry differ from the rules for quoting fiction and drama. Because line endings are meaningful in poetry, you indicate them with a slash when incorporating quotations into your prose. Double slashes indicate stanza breaks. Line numbers, rather than page numbers, appear in parentheses after the quotation and before the final period. For example:

The speaker's father looms large in her imagination; to her he is a "Ghastly statue with one gray toe / Big as a Frisco seal // And a head in the freakish Atlantic" (9-11).

If you are quoting more than three lines, introduce them and then present them starting on a new line, indented one inch. Do not add quotation marks; setting the lines off from your paragraph has already signalled their status as quoted material. Double space. Place the parenthetical reference after the quotation (outside any quoted punctuation). An example:

```
The first stanza of Plath's "Daddy" establishes a
pattern of assonance which is sustained throughout
the poem:

    You do not do, you do not do
    Any more, black shoe
    In which I have lived like a foot
    For thirty years, poor and white,
    Barely daring to breathe or Achoo. (1-5)
```

Where the spatial arrangement of a poem is meaningful, reproduce it in your quotation. Here's an example featuring concrete poetry.

```
Cummings's placement of letters forces the reader's
eye to leap in tandem with the grasshopper:
    aThe):l
            eA
             !p:
    S                                               a
                         (r
                                              (7-11)
```

Secondary Sources

It's important to strike the right balance when incorporating the statements of other critics into your essay. If your research paper does not include enough, it can come off as vague, unconvincing, or not fully engaged with the relevant critical dialogue out there. If you quote too many other critics, you risk obscuring your own position. If you don't offer a thoughtful response to the quotations you include, your essay can read like a patchwork quilt.

Include the secondary quotations that really propel your own discussion. An effective quotation might express a key point you wish to elaborate on or, alternatively, introduce a thesis with which you strongly disagree. Direct quotations in these cases efficiently establish a platform from which to launch your original position.

When quoting a critic in your essay, integrate short quotations smoothly into your own prose, citing page number parenthetically. If you include the author's name in your text, there's no need to repeat it in parentheses, but if you do not include it in your text, supply it in parentheses. Here are examples of both:

> Wendy Martin suggests that Rich's feminism is embodied in "a comprehensive vision of life which honors all people" (163).

> The feminism of Adrienne Rich has been described as "a comprehensive vision of life which honors all people" (Martin 163).

If a quotation runs longer than four lines, start on a new line, indented one inch, double spaced. Parenthetical page reference follows the final period. Longer quotations are usually introduced with a colon. Here's an example:

> Dilworth concludes his argument by proposing "Ode on a Grecian Urn" as a joint project:

> > This is not to say that the ode is merely a rewriting of Shakespeare's poem. Keats gives as well as he gets, and, especially by making the urn "Grecian" (with depictions on its outer surface), transforms the Shakespearean material so that it now belongs, in another paradox, as much to Keats as to Shakespeare. Is there any comparable example in literature of such complete yet subtle 'collaboration' (posthumous on Shakespeare's part) between two so supremely gifted poets?
> >
> > (p. 59)

Works Cited

Again, you can consult the *MLA Handbook for Writers of Research Papers* to determine how to cite all manner of different sources, but here are the basics:

Your Works Cited list appears at the end of your essay, starting on a new page. Entries are presented alphabetically by last name. After the first line, flush with the left margin, indent half an inch. Double-space.

A print book:

Last name, First name. *Title of Book*. Place of publication: Publisher, Year of Publication. Print.

e.g.,

Christakos, Margaret. *Multitudes*. Toronto: Coach House P, 2013. Print.

A poem within a book:

Last name, First name. "Title of poem." *Title of Book*. Place of publication: Publisher, Year of Publication. Page number(s). Print.

e.g.,

Christakos, Margaret. "Late One Night." *Multitudes*. Toronto: Coach House P, 2013. 38. Print.

A poem within an anthology:

Last name, First name. "Title of poem." *Title of Anthology*. Ed. Name(s) of editor(s). Place of publication: Publisher, Date. Page number(s). Print.

e.g.,

Dickinson, Emily. "A narrow Fellow in the Grass." *The Broadview Anthology of Poetry*. Ed. Herbert Rosengarten and Amanda Goldrick-Jones. Peterborough, ON: Broadview P, 1993. 322. Print.

A poem from print book accessed on the web:

Last name, First name. "Title of poem." *Title of Book*. Place of publication: Publisher, Year of Publication. *Title of Website*. Web. Date of access.
e.g.,

Keats, John. "Ode to a Nightingale." *The Poetical Works of John Keats*. Ed. Francis T. Palgrave. London: MacMillan, 1884. 213-15. *Bartleby.com*. Web. 25 October 2013.

An article in a print journal:

Last name, First name. "Title of article." *Name of Journal* Volume. Issue number (year): page numbers. Print.
e.g.,

Mix, Deborah. "Tender Revisions: Harryette Mullen's *Trimmings* and *S*PeRM**K*T*." *American Literature* 77 (2005): 65-92. Print.

A print article accessed on the Web:

Last name, First name. "Title of article." *Name of Journal* Volume. Issue number (year): page numbers. *Title of Website*. Web. Date of access.
e.g.,

Miner, Paul. "'The Tyger': Genesis & Evolution in the Poetry of William Blake." *Criticism* 4.1 (Winter 1962): 59-73. *JSTOR*. Web. 27 January 2015.

If you cite two or more works by the same author, use three hyphens to stand for their name after the first appearance:

Rich, Adrienne. "Aunt Jennifer's Tigers." *A Change of World*. New Haven: Yale UP, 1951. 19. Print.

---. Interview. *The Language of Life: A Festival of Poets*. By Bill Moyers. New York: Broadway Books, 1995. 335-53. Print.

If you cite two or more works from the same anthology, cross-reference entries to a full citation of the collection. Cross-referenced works then need only mention the editor(s) and page number:

Blake, William. "The Lamb." Rosengarten and Goldrick-Jones 155.
---. "The Tyger." Rosengarten and Goldrick-Jones 157-58.
Hopkins, Gerard Manley. "God's Grandeur." Rosengarten and Goldrick-Jones 348.
Rosengarten, Herbert and Amanda Goldrick-Jones, eds. *The Broadview Anthology of Poetry*. Peterborough, ON: Broadview P, 1993. Print.

Below is the final version of Jacob's essay.

Jacob Young
Dr. Susan Holbrook
26-120(2)
26 March 2014

The Hammer is a Needle:
Adrienne Rich Answers William Blake

Poet and essayist Adrienne Rich was one of the most important feminist voices in America. "Aunt Jennifer's Tigers," one of her early poems, offers a critique of marriage in a patriarchal society. Published in 1951, the poem portrays a woman who bears "the massive weight of Uncle's wedding band" (7), an image recalled three lines later when she is described as a woman "*ringed* (emphasis added) with ordeals she was mastered by" (10). As unlike Aunt Jennifer as possible are the proud and brave tigers she has embroidered. The contrast between the woman and her creations lends the poem energy. Several critics have suggested that the tigers are an allusion to the beast in Blake's famous poem

"The Tyger." Cheri Colby Langdell, for instance, argues that Rich's choice of animal magnifies the differences between Aunt Jennifer and her art, stating, "The tigers' aesthetic energy, taking on a symbolic dimension and energy from William Blake's "Tyger," contrasts sharply with Aunt Jennifer's inner fears, her outer silence, and submissiveness" (26). I suggest that the intertextual connection is even more profound, and therefore the feminist message more radical.

In both overt and subtle ways, the poet underscores the difference between the tigers and Aunt Jennifer. The tigers are "unafraid" (12) and, more specifically, they "do not fear the men" (3), whereas as Aunt Jennifer has "terrified hands" (9). The two most prominent instances of alliteration in the poem serve to differentiate the figures. The tigers are "prancing, proud" (12), the plosive 'p' a forceful sound. Aunt Jennifer possesses "fingers fluttering" (5), featuring a soft fricative. These consonant sounds convey a distinct difference in character, in energy; the plosive recalls a popping balloon, while the fricative sounds more like a balloon's slow deflation. Rich's polarization of figures in the poem is aided in no small part by the spectre of Blake's canonical tigers. Blake's poem, however, is more than a striking portrait. It is also a variously repeated urgent question: "What immortal hand or eye / Dare frame thy fearful symmetry?" (23-24). Blake's speaker wants to know who could have created such an awe-inspiring beast. I argue that Adrienne Rich's poem furnishes that question with an answer: Aunt Jennifer.

"The Tyger" occupied a special place in the imagination of Adrienne Rich. In an interview with Bill Moyers, she recalls encountering it as a child:

> Moyers: Do you remember the first poem that touched you deeply, that awakened you somehow?
> Rich: I think it was Blake's "The Tyger." I was

given poems to copy, that was how my father
taught me to do handwriting. "The Tyger" was one
of them and it was so musical and mysterious.
The wonderful image sank very deep very early.
(347)

It is not surprising that Blake should supply the image
electrifying Rich's poem and that, further, "Aunt
Jennifer's Tigers" might be seen as a response to his
burning question. That the Rich work offers an answer
to Blake is supported by formal resonances between the
two. The stanza form of both poems is the quatrain.
Both poems are comprised of rhyming couplets. The
second line of Blake's poem states the tigers' habitat
"in the forests of the night;" Rich follows suit, her
second line celebrating the "Bright topaz denizens of
a world of green." Note in that line the word "Bright,"
recalling Blake's famous opening: "Tyger! Tyger! burning
bright."

Other points of resonance between the poems relate
more specifically to my thesis that Rich's poem supplies
a response to Blake's question. "The Tyger" is really
consumed with the creator of the beast rather than the
beast itself. The word "hand" appears four times in
the poem. The speaker wonders "what dread grasp" (15)
could "frame" (4), "seize" (8) and "clasp" (16) in
the creation of the formidable tiger. In Rich's poem
we see corresponding references to "Aunt Jennifer's
hand" (8), "her terrified hands" (9) and those "fingers
fluttering." Blake's speaker muses about this creator's
tools, imagining a "hammer," a "chain" (13) and an
"anvil" (15). Rich puts these speculations to rest
with a surprising answer; the tigers were made with an
"ivory needle" (6). To Blake's incredulous question,
"Did he who made the Lamb make thee?" (20), Rich's poem
responds in the affirmative, a 'yes' subtly suggested
in the "wool" (5) Aunt Jennifer is using. While most

critics focus on the contrast between Aunt Jennifer
and her embroidered tigers, close investigation of the
poem alongside its Blakean intertext reveals another
fruitful axis of comparison, that between Blake's
imagined creator and Rich's unassuming Aunt Jennifer.
To the question of what an artist, a writer, a creator
looks like, Rich presents Aunt Jennifer. Even under
the duress of patriarchy, women have managed to
create. Women's artistic expression has been sometimes
constrained, sometimes consigned solely to 'feminine'
media such as needlework, sometimes delivered under
a pseudonym, sometimes gone unseen/unread, but the
creative spirit has endured. Whether we are thinking in
terms of the human or the divine, our image of creator
has been limited by androcentrism.

Just as "The Tyger" can be read in part as Blake's
interrogation of his own creative power, "Aunt Jennifer's
Tigers" engages Rich's fraught position as a writer.
In her 1971 essay, "When we Dead Awaken: Writing as
Revision," Rich recalls writing the poem: "I thought I
was creating a portrait of an imaginary woman. But this
woman suffers from the opposition of her imagination,
worked out in tapestry, and her life-style, 'ringed
with ordeals she was mastered by'" (40). Later in life
it is clear to her that this figure was a refraction
of Rich herself, a young woman torn between artistic
ambition and societal expectations. The poem appeared
in her first collection, A Change of World, auspiciously
introduced by W.H. Auden. But his introduction bears the
stamp of the chauvinism of his era. Auden praises the
book: "…the poems a reader will encounter in this book
are neatly and modestly dressed, speak quietly but do
not mumble, respect their elders but are not cowed by
them, and do not tell fibs…" (11). It is hard to imagine
such a patronizing statement passing for praise of a
male poet. To launch into the sexist cultural climate of
the 1950's a poem like "Aunt Jennifer's Tigers," a poem

that dares to take on Blake in the championing of female creativity, was a great feminist intervention.

While my argument is bolstered by Rich's childhood intimacy with "The Tyger," and by the multiple echoes between the two poems, I don't argue that she herself would claim the poem was deliberately composed as a direct response to Blake. Her recollection of the poem in "When we Dead Awaken" mentions nothing of the Romantic poet. But as we know, poetry tends to exceed the conscious grasp of even its authors; upon her realization that the poem was more about herself than she could admit at the time, she muses, "But poems are like dreams: in them you put what you don't know you know" (40). Spoken like someone fully compelled by the challenges, gifts, and mysteries of creativity; how fitting that in blurbing Rich's 1995 collection, *Dark Fields of the Republic*, Nadine Gordimer should declare, "Adrienne Rich is the Blake of American Letters."

Works Cited

Auden, W. H. Foreword. *A Change of World*. By Adrienne
    Rich. New Haven: Yale U P, 1951. 7-11. Print.

Blake, William. "The Tyger." *The Broadview Anthology of
    Poetry*. Ed. Herbert Rosengarten and Amanda Goldrick-
    Jones. Peterborough, ON: Broadview P, 1993. 157-58.
    Print.

Gordimer, Nadine. Back cover blurb for *Dark Fields of
    the Republic: Poems, 1991-1995*. By Adrienne Rich. New
    York: W. W. Norton & Company, 1995.

Langdell, Cheri Colby. *Adrienne Rich: The Moment of
    Change*. Westport, CT: Praeger-Greenwood, 2004. Print.

Rich, Adrienne. "Aunt Jennifer's Tigers." *A Change of
    World*. New Haven: Yale U P, 1951. 19. Print.

---. Interview. *The Language of Life: A Festival of
    Poets*. By Bill Moyers. New York: Broadway Books,
    1995. 335-53. Print.

---. "When we Dead Awaken: Writing as Revision." *Lies,
    Secrets, and Silence: Selected Prose 1966-1978*. New
    York: W. W. Norton & Company, 1979. 33-49. Print.

A NOTE ON PLAGIARISM: Don't do it! Every year I have the unpleasant experience of reading plagiarized material in a student essay. With so much critical discussion at our fingertips via the internet, some find it pretty tempting to cut and paste a few passages, especially when it's 3 a.m. and the assignment is due that day.

I'm going to go out on a limb here and assume, based on your reading of this very sentence, that you would not consciously pass someone else's work off as your own. But even you need to be very careful about inadvertently plagiarizing. The key is to document your sources. If you quote another critic directly, you'll use quotation marks and a parenthetical reference. It's such a shame when a student does all that good research, only to face a charge of plagiarism because of sketchy attribution. You should be proud of the research you've done: quote, cite source, and engage in dialogue with the critics you've read.

Because your own analysis and your secondary research are being carried out in tandem, you risk accidental plagiarism. For example, when taking down some notes on a critic's essay, you'll experience some aha! moments inspired by their analysis; you'll want to disagree with them, perhaps, or you'll jump off one of their points. Later, when you look at your notes, you might forget which observations were yours and which were the critic's. A simple way to prevent this confusion: at the top of the page, write the full bibliographic information for the article you're studying; as you're reading, use point form (-) when paraphrasing the critic; use quotation marks when recording one of their points word-for-word (" "); and enclose in square brackets ([ ]) any original insight you have as you are going along. That way, when you consult your notes while composing the essay, you can be confident of proper attribution, and distinguish your own important voice from others in the critical conversation.

Glossary of Poetic Terms

ACCENTUAL-SYLLABIC VERSE The dominant system of meter since the Renaissance: lines of poetry composed according to both regular stress patterns and syllable counts.

ACCENTUAL VERSE Accentual verse features consistency in the number of accents, or stresses, per line. The number of unaccented syllables is irregular. This system of meter has been in use from the beginnings of English poetry, although overshadowed by accentual-syllabic meter since the Renaissance. It has persisted in popular forms, such as folk ballads and nursery rhymes.

ALEXANDRINE Uncommon in English poetry, a line of iambic hexameter is often termed an alexandrine. The alexandrine was for centuries the dominant verse form in French poetry, its twelve syllables divided up variously over time, but usually featuring four stresses.

ALLEGORY A narrative or image which can be understood on a surface level as well as on a metaphorical level.

ALLITERATION Repeated consonant sounds appearing at the beginning of words or stressed syllables.

ALLUSION A passing reference to another cultural text (literary, mythological, cinematic, etc.) or to a historical figure or event.

ANACRUSIS One or more unaccented syllables falling at the beginning of a line and not counted as part of the poem's established metrical pattern.

ANAPHORA Repetition of a word or phrase, usually at the beginning of a line. This figure can achieve various effects. In Walt Whitman's "When I

Heard the Learn'd Astronomer" (p. 93), for instance, it functions in the first four lines to underscore the scientist's incessant lecturing and the speaker's growing restlessness.

APOSTROPHE An address to an absent person, thing, or abstraction.

ASSONANCE Same or similar vowel sounds repeated in close proximity.

AVANT-GARDE French for "advance guard," the term is used in the arts to describe creative people, movements, and works that are experimental, pushing beyond the limits of established norms.

BALLAD Flourishing in the Renaissance period, the traditional English folk ballad was a simple narrative song, transmitted orally, featuring rhymed quatrain stanzas with alternating tetrameter and trimeter lines. The subject matter was commonly tragic, drawn from local history, delivered in the impersonal third person and reflective of popular cultural worldviews rather than an individual perspective. The form has persisted, as we can see in Countee Cullen's "Tableau" (p. 21) and Emily Dickinson's "A narrow Fellow in the Grass" (p. 62).

BLANK VERSE Unrhymed lines of iambic pentameter. The most widely used verse form in traditional English poetry. Blank verse is the dominant form in Shakespeare's plays. We also find it in Milton's *Paradise Lost* (1667) and Wordsworth's *Prelude* (1850).

BLAZON Popularized by Petrarch, the blazon is a commonplace of Renaissance love poetry in which the speaker enumerates and celebrates the various virtues, primarily physical, of his beloved.

CAESURA A grammatical pause mid-line, often marked by a period, semicolon, or comma.

CANON Originally the term referred to a body of texts considered to be authentic; for example, the Shakespeare canon is the group of works critics have agreed are genuine products of Shakespeare's hand. Now the term is used more often to refer to a body of writings considered to be the best and most important literary accomplishments of a nation, an era, a genre, etc. An introductory survey course of British Literature, for instance, would likely include Shakespeare, because he is so firmly entrenched in the canon. Over the past few decades, critics have become increasingly aware of how cultural biases shape literary canons. As a result, received canons are subject to intervention and expansion, including, for example, more women authors and authors of colour.

CARPE DIEM Latin phrase meaning "seize the day." Appearing originally in Horace's *Odes*, *carpe diem* has become a shorthand way to refer to the perennial theme, especially prevalent in love poetry, of embracing pleasure while one can in this short life. In Elizabethan poetry, this urgent plea is often expressed by a speaker attempting to persuade a chaste young woman to submit to advances. The most famous poetic expression of *carpe diem* is Marvell's "To His Coy Mistress."

CATALECTIC In a catalectic line, a final syllable that would normally fulfil the established meter has been dropped. The noun form is CATALEXIS.

CHIASMUS A figure of speech in which the second half reverses the terms of the first. From the Greek letter 'chi', inscribed as an X. E.g., "When the going gets tough, the tough get going."

CONCRETE POETRY This mode of poetry makes the most of language as physical material. Pattern poems, which have been around at least since the third century BCE, are organized so that the overall shape of the poem echoes its subject matter. George Herbert's altar-shaped poem "The Altar" is an example from the Renaissance period. But concrete poetry embraces more than simply shape poems; the term, popularized in the 1950s during a surge of experimental output on an international scale, applies to a wide range of innovative poetry that engages the physicality of language, even down to the level of the letter and punctuation. See bp Nichol's "Blues" (p. 1). While definitions shift and overlap, the expression "concrete poetry" in its most generous scope embraces pattern poetry, visual poetry, sound poetry, and new digital forms.

CONFESSIONAL POETRY A mode of poetry first identified by M.L. Rosenthal in 1959 in a review of American poet Robert Lowell's *Life Studies*, confessional poetry is more revealing and detailed in its expression of the self than the poetry that came before. Poets commonly associated with this mode include Sylvia Plath, John Berryman, and Anne Sexton.

CONSONANCE Same or similar consonant sounds repeated in close proximity. Alliteration (see above) is a form of consonance.

DACTYLIC METER A meter composed of the following repeated foot: stressed syllable + two unstressed syllables (´ ˘ ˘).

DECONSTRUCTION A theory and practice of literary criticism that proceeds from the notion that language itself is an infinitely unsettled system, so that literary texts cannot be the closed, unified, articulable systems we might presume them to be. Deconstructive interpretations seek to unveil in a work the inconsistencies, contradictions and alternate paths of meaning that are always unresolvable. The principal theorist of deconstruction was Jacques Derrida (1930–2004), whose interest was in all kinds of language, indeed in the philosophical underpinnings of our culture. Critics more specifically focussed on literature, however, popularized deconstruction as a productive and revolutionary way to explore the instability of textual dynamics.

DICTION The choice of vocabulary and phrasing in a work, contributing to its tonal effect. For example, a poem can come across as formal, casual, lofty, or playful thanks to the poet's choice of diction.

EKPHRASTIC POEM An ekphrastic poem responds to another, non-literary, work, usually a sculpture or painting. E.g., Keats's "Ode on a Grecian Urn."

ELEGY A formal poem of lament, usually mourning the death of an individual. An important subtype is the pastoral elegy, originated by the ancient Greeks and revived in the Renaissance; the pastoral elegy features shepherds in a Classical rustic setting.

ELISON The suppression of a vowel or syllable, often to accommodate a metrical scheme.

END RHYME Rhyme occurring among the terminal words of lines.

ENJAMBMENT The carrying over of sense and syntax from the end of one line to the beginning of the next. Literally (from the French *enjambement*) "a straddling." An enjambed line is also referred to as a run-on line.

EPIC A long narrative poem detailing the adventures of a hero or heroes. The epic form has a long history; the earliest surviving example is *Gilgamesh* (c. 3000 BCE). Homer's *Iliad* and *Odyssey* are key epics in the Western canon, arising out of an oral narrative tradition. Later epic works often adopt conventions seen in Homer, such as the inaugural invocation of a muse and beginning *in medias res* (in the middle of things).

EPITHALAMION (ALSO EPITHALAMIUM) A poem written in celebration of a marriage. Originated by Classical poets, the form was taken up with enthusiasm by poets of the Renaissance. Most famous is Edmund Spenser's "Epithalamion" (1595).

EUPHONY A sonically pleasing quality. A euphonic phrase, thanks to letter combinations and rhythmic profile, is attractive to the ear and generally easy to pronounce.

FEMININE ENDING An unstressed terminal syllable.

FOOT The repeated metrical unit in a line of verse, for example an iamb or dactyl.

FREE VERSE The majority of modern and contemporary poetry is written in free verse; unlike most poetry composed before the twentieth century, free verse does not adhere to any fixed meter or rhyme scheme. Sound and rhythm usually remain of prime importance in free verse, and patterns appear, but these are unique and organic to the individual poem rather than predetermined.

HAIKU A short, unrhymed Japanese poem which recounts and invites a moment of acute perception and meditation. Natural imagery figures prominently. As adopted by English language practitioners, the haiku usually appears in three lines, with the following syllable counts: 5,7,5. Early twentieth-century poets, exploring the potential of free verse, were particularly interested in haiku, a concise form free of regular rhyme and meter.

HARLEM RENAISSANCE The explosion of creative and intellectual activity among African Americans between the end of World War I and the Great Depression. New York's Harlem neighbourhood was the hub of this energetic flowering, which both celebrated African American heritage and produced innovative new work across the arts, establishing a firm foothold for blacks in the greater American cultural landscape.

HERESY OF PARAPHRASE This term was introduced by Cleanth Brooks in *The Well Wrought Urn* (1947). Brooks argued that one cannot paraphrase, or put into other words, the full meaning of a poem. We fall into the trap of this heresy ourselves when we claim "What the poet is really saying is ..." or "What the poet is trying to say is ...," as if poetry were either a needless obfuscation or a sketchy form of communication. Brooks invited readers to consider poetry as they would the other arts, such as ballet or painting, as "an experience rather than any mere statement about experience or any mere abstraction from experience" (213).

HEROIC COUPLET A rhyming pair of iambic pentameter lines (see below), the heroic couplet was especially popular during the eighteenth century. Alexander Pope wrote the majority of his works in heroic couplets.

HYPERBOLE Exaggeration, overstatement. The speaker in Sylvia Plath's "Daddy" describes her father's toe as "Big as a Frisco seal." Nobody's toe could be this large; the hyperbole helps convey the space her father occupies in her psyche.

IAMBIC METER A meter composed of the following repeated foot: unstressed syllable + stressed syllable (˘ ´). This foot is called an IAMB.

IAMBIC PENTAMETER Lines comprising five iambic feet (see above). One of the most commonly employed meters in English poetry.

IMAGERY A vague and variable but ubiquitous term in literary criticism. Imagery generally refers to the non-abstract elements in a poem, particularly those evoking a mental picture, but also those offering other sense-impressions (e.g., of sound, taste, touch).

INDETERMINACY Undecidability of meaning, the unstable link between text and referent. Critic Marjorie Perloff, in *The Poetics of Indeterminacy* (1981), popularized the term in poetry circles to characterize a body of work in which the connections among words on the page, rather than connections between words and their referents, are foregrounded. Poems by Gertrude Stein (pp. 39, 63, 93) exemplify the energy of indeterminacy.

INTENTIONAL FALLACY This term was coined by New Critics W.K. Wimsatt Jr. and Monroe C. Beardsley to name what they argued is the misguided assumption that a work's meaning resides within the scope of the author's intentions. While these intentions (whether stated or divined) can be instructive and interesting, the meaning and import of a text continues to evolve as it passes through different cultural contexts, different critical climates, and different readers' hands. Even at the moment of composition an author can be aware of neither the unconscious forces within his or her own process, nor the full interplay between the text and its contemporary social milieu.

INTERTEXTUALITY A resonant relationship between texts. Intertextuality is manifested through citation, allusion, echoing, borrowing, parody, etc. The relationship can be macro—Millay's sonnets bear an intertextual connection to the entire sonnet tradition—or micro, as when Anne Bradstreet invokes the works of Du Bartas in "Prologue." Taken to its logical limits, intertextuality is the condition of all texts; as deconstruction (see above) has shown, all words are understood only through their relationships with other words (through difference, repetition, improvisation, etc.).

IRONY There are many subcategories of irony useful to the literary critic, a number of which apply to poetry. In verbal irony (which is akin to, though more subtle than, sarcasm), the words of a speaker contradict his or her true feelings or intentions. A poem might also make use of a naïve persona, which would effect structural irony; more commonly encountered in fiction, such a speaker expresses sentiments different from those of the author, with whom we are invited to more closely identify. More importantly, the critical and nuanced disposition poets have toward all language imbues poetry with a kind of charge somewhere in the domain of these expressive ironies. Consider the difference, for example, between the way one might approach the word "love" or "democracy" in a poem and the way one would read it in a newspaper article. There's occasion in poetry, of course, to discover irony in its more general sense, too. In common parlance, the term is usually applied to instances of situational irony, in which expectations are dramatically dashed in a manner often involving a paradox or contradiction. (Note: Alanis Morissette's song "Ironic" misuses the term; if there's "rain on your wedding day," that's just unfortunate rather than ironic. If it rains on your wedding day and you are a meteorologist and your new spouse is a wedding planner, that's pretty ironic).

LINEATION The organization of poetry into lines (as opposed to the arbitrary termination of lines of text determined by page margin, as in prose).

LYRIC A relatively brief poem featuring a single speaker expressing thoughts and feelings. The lyric appears in many forms, including the sonnet, ode and free verse. In ancient Greece the lyric was a poem sung to the accompaniment of a lyre. Since the Romantic period, it has become the dominant poetic mode.

MASCULINE ENDING A stressed terminal syllable.

METAPHOR A figure of speech comparing one thing to another; unlike a simile, a metaphor does not flag the analogy with, for example, "like" or "as." Although we see intensive and innovative use of metaphor in poetry, it is a feature of all language use (see my use of "flag" in the previous sentence!).

METAPHYSICAL CONCEIT A conceit is an extended, often elaborate metaphor. A metaphysical conceit is so named because the group of seventeenth-century poets termed the metaphysical poets (John Donne principal among them) excelled at these complex, sometimes outrageous, rhetorical figures. For example, in Donne's "A Valediction: Forbidding Mourning," the speaker likens his soul and that of his lover to the legs of a compass; this imaginative comparison is sustained over three stanzas, the interdependent movements of the two legs serving to highlight the connection between the lovers.

METER The pattern of recurring units of speech-sound, such as accented and unaccented syllables. If the ten-syllable lines of a poem are each built of five units: unstressed syllable + stressed syllable, for example, we can say the poem is composed in iambic pentameter. Meter is a more specific term than rhythm. See *A Brief Guide to Meter* (p. 111).

METONYMY A figure of speech in which a word stands for an object or concept to which it is related. "Crown" is a metonym for the monarchy, for example, and "Beethoven" is a metonym for the music of Beethoven. The metonymic relationship is more intimate than connections possible in metaphor (a figure through which wildly diverse objects can be compared). Synecdoche is a category of metonymy in which a part stands for the whole; e.g., using "hand" to indicate a worker.

NEGATIVE CAPABILITY Introduced by Romantic poet John Keats in a letter to his brothers in 1817, this term has reverberated for critics and poets ever since. Keats describes negative capability as a state in which someone is "capable of being in uncertainties, mysteries, doubts, without any irritable reaching after fact and reason," and notes that Shakespeare had it in spades. The idea has been variously interpreted and adopted, taken to point to, for example, the egolessness of the ideal poet, and the special status of poetry as existing in the realm of beauty and therefore impervious to concerns of logic and evidence. Keats's letter continues on the subject of great poets, for whom "the sense of Beauty overcomes every other consideration, or rather obliterates all consideration" (*Letters* 48). For readers the term offers an appealing way to describe the experience of enjoying a difficult poem; we can at once be in a state of continued puzzlement and enduring pleasure.

NEOLOGISM A newly invented word, or word introduced from another language. In the absence of a word that can express precisely what they mean, poets create new words; to suggest the incomparable beauty of the Northern Lights, for example, Emily Dickinson coined "competeless" ("Of Bronze — and Blaze —"), and to capture the exquisite joy of youth and Spring, E.E. Cummings invented new compound words "mud-luscious" and "puddle-wonderful" ("in Just-"). New technologies often necessitate neologisms: the verb 'to Google' has now entered our lexicon.

NEW CRITICISM A school of literary criticism dominating the field during the mid-twentieth century. New Critics steered focus away from historical and biographical concerns, arguing for the autonomy of the text itself. Their detailed attention to the internal workings of a poem inaugurated a practice of close reading, or explication, which forever influenced the practice of literary criticism. In New Criticism, interpretations of successful poems tended to focus on tensions, paradox, and irony, and how these ultimately resolve into some kind of unity. This view of poems as complex yet closed systems was challenged in the 1960s by critics who became more interested in the open, unresolved, nature of poetry, as well as in the contexts of its production and reception. Two key New Critical texts are John Crowe Ransom's *The New Criticism* (1941) and Cleanth Brooks's *The Well Wrought Urn* (1947).

NEW HISTORICISM A mode of literary criticism that views creative texts as inseparable from their historical contexts. New Historicist critics see literary works as both reflective of and productive of the worldviews of their contemporary milieus. Stephen Greenblatt—author of numerous acclaimed books, including *Renaissance Self-Fashioning* (1980), *Shakespearean Negotiations* (1988), and *The Swerve: How the World Became Modern* (2011)—is the pioneering figure of this critical movement.

OCTAVE A grouping of eight lines. Most commonly used in reference to the first eight lines of a Petrarchan sonnet, with a rhyme scheme of *abbaabba*.

ODE A lyric poem celebrating, and often addressed to, a person, thing, or abstraction, with a tone that is elevated, serious. There are three principal forms: the Pindaric ode (original choral Greek form, public; rare in English), the Horatian ode (from Roman poet Horace; more personal in tone), and the Cowleyan (after Renaissance poet Abraham Cowley; also called "irregular").

ONOMATOPOEIA A word that sonically imitates its meaning. E.g., buzz, clap, crunch.

OTTAVA RIMA An eight-line iambic pentameter stanza, with the rhyme scheme *abababcc*. Adapted from Italian epic poetry (it originated with fourteenth-century poet Boccaccio), ottava rima appears in, for example, Byron's *Don Juan* (1819) and W.B. Yeats's "Sailing to Byzantium" (1928).

OXYMORON A figure of speech yoking contradictory terms, e.g., burning ice, honest thief. An oxymoron is a condensed form of paradox (see below).

PARADOX A statement which is seemingly illogical or contradictory, often reconcilable upon reflection. Wordsworth warns of the paradoxical "weight of too much liberty" in his celebration of the constraining yet comforting sonnet form ("Prefatory Sonnet"). Emily Dickinson opens her most famous poem about fame with the paradox "I'm Nobody."

PASTORAL A mode of literature featuring the idealized, simple life of shepherds in a beautiful rustic setting. Poets of ancient Greece and Rome (notably Theocritus and Virgil) developed the pastoral, and it was revived in the Renaissance.

PATHETIC FALLACY Victorian critic John Ruskin (1819-1900) coined this term to identify what he deemed the falsifying practice of attributing human characteristics to inanimate elements of Nature (e.g., suggesting that sunshine smiles or clouds cry). Critics continue to use the term, but generally not in a derogatory manner.

PERSONA Technically interchangeable with 'speaker,' in practice critics tend to prefer persona when the voice of the poem is clearly distinct from that of the author. This usage is consonant with the Latin term's original meaning: mask, character.

PERSONIFICATION The attribution of human characteristics to objects, nonhuman creatures, and abstractions.

PROSE POEM A poem in which lineation does not play a significant role. Prose poems trouble the boundaries between prose and poetry, combining the energies of the sentence/paragraph and the intensive music, figurative language, and disjunctions associated with poetry.

QUATRAIN A grouping of four lines. The traditional ballad, for example, features quatrain stanzas. The Shakespearean sonnet comprises three quatrains (distinguished by the rhyme scheme) and a rhyming couplet.

READER-RESPONSE CRITICISM This form of literary criticism highlights the role of readers in the development of meaning and in the long-term cultural evaluation of a literary work. Such a stance recognizes the differences among readers and the consequent multiplicity of a text's possible interpretations.

RENAISSANCE Also termed the Early Modern period, the Renaissance (literally 're-birth') was the era following the Middle Ages. Across Europe this period (c. 1400-1650) saw a revival of Classical literature and an explosion of scholarly activity and new artistic production. The invention of the movable type printing press by Gutenberg in the mid-fifteenth century facilitated these pursuits. This period also saw the rise of individualism, the Copernican revolution, and the discovery by Europeans of the so-called New World.

RHYME The repetition of same or similar sounds (a combination of vowel and consonants), e.g., far/star. There are many sub-varieties, such as end rhyme (see definition above), eye rhyme (words bearing similar spelling but different sound, e.g., bear/hear), slant rhyme (inexact duplication, e.g., mother/rather), internal rhyme (two or more words rhyming within a line) and feminine rhyme (involving two or more syllables, e.g., wither/slither).

RHYMING COUPLET A pair of end-rhymed lines. Shakespeare's sonnets conclude with a rhyming couplet. Rhyming couplets can appear alone as pithy epigrams, or in lengthy sequences, as in Chaucer's *The Canterbury Tales* (1476). Rhymed couplets in iambic pentameter are also called heroic couplets.

RHYTHM is a more general term than meter. It can refer to the overall beat structure of a work, often shaped by an underlying meter but including all variations and deviations. It can also be used to talk about an interesting passage that does not adhere to any standard meter. All poems have a rhythm, but not all poems have a regular meter. We can talk about the rhythms in free verse, speech, music, or falling rain.

ROMANTIC ERA Critics generally date this period between the late-eighteenth and mid-nineteenth centuries. A few concepts associated with the English Romantic poets include the importance of feeling and its uncensored expression; the artist as original genius; the creative power of imagination; interest in folk culture; the breaking free of inherited forms, rules, and ideas; and the primacy of wild Nature, which is linked to the spiritual realm.

SAPIR-WHORF HYPOTHESIS Named after American linguistic anthropologists Benjamin Lee Whorf (1897-1941) and his mentor Edward Sapir (1884-1939), who explored the notion of linguistic relativity—that is, the idea that a person's particular language affects his or her patterns of cognition and behaviour.

SCAN When you scan a poem, you are determining its meter by analyzing patterns of stressed and unstressed syllables, marking them with symbols such as the ictus: ´ (for stressed) and breve: ˘ (for unstressed). Metrical feet (the recurring units) are delineated by vertical bars. Scanning also involves noting caesurae and rhyme schemes, the former with the symbol: || and the latter with letters of the alphabet. The noun form is SCANSION.

SESTET A grouping of six lines. Most commonly used to refer to the final six lines of a Petrarchan sonnet. The sestet begins with a volta, or turn in the argument of the poem. Rhyme scheme is traditionally *cdecde*, but can vary.

SESTINA A seven-stanza poetic form of French origin, in which the final words of each line get repeated in varying orders. So if the first line ends with the word "love," "love" will appear at the end of a line in each of the subsequent five stanzas. These first six stanzas are comprised of six lines each. The final stanza (termed an envoi) features three lines, also ending in three of the earlier terminal words (and often including the other three mid-line). The sestina pattern adheres to a rule that the final word of one stanza concludes the first line of the following stanza. The pleasure of reading sestinas arises in part from appreciating the elegant compositional contortionism the form requires.

SIMILE A figure of speech comparing someone or something to something else. Unlike metaphors, similes are clearly marked by the use of "like" or "as."

SONNET From the Italian *sonetto* (a little sound or song). A poem comprised of fourteen iambic pentameter lines, traditionally featuring a single speaker expressing love or admiration and/or reflecting on his own feelings. Developed during the late Middle Ages, sonnets were popularized by the Italian poet Francesco Petrarca (Petrarch) and adopted by English poets during the sixteenth century. For more on the difference between Petrarchan (or Italian) and Shakespearean (or English) sonnets, see p. 10. The form has endured since its inception, and continues as a locus of poetic expression, innovation and experimentation to this day. See BLAZON.

SPEAKER The constructed voice of a lyric poem. Important as a distinction from the author, who may have nothing in common with the speaking voice of the work. Comparable to the narrator in fiction. See PERSONA.

STANZA A grouping of lines constituting a section in a poem, set off from others by spacing. From the Italian for 'room,' or 'stopping place.'

SYMBOL More resonant and complex than an image, a symbol is replete with significance, either as a cultural repository of accrued meaning (e.g., a cross, a rose), or as developed within the limited world of an author's *oeuvre* or a single literary work.

SYNECDOCHE See METONYMY.

SYNTAX The arrangement of grammatical elements in a phrase, line, or sentence.

TERZA RIMA A form composed of tercets (three-line stanzas) interlinked through rhyme: the rhyme of lines 1 and 3 is carried down from line 2 of the previous stanza (*aba bcb cbc*, etc.). The most famous composition in terza rima is Dante's *Divine Comedy*. The form rarely appears in English, which is (relative to Italian) rhyme-poor. A well-known English example is Percy Bysshe Shelley's "Ode to the West Wind."

TONE Mood, feeling, atmosphere. A discussion of tone might refer to the overall effect of a poem, or specifically to the voice of a speaker.

TROCHAIC METER A meter composed of the following repeated foot: stressed syllable + unstressed syllable (´ ˘).

VOLTA A turn in the argument of a Petrarchan sonnet, appearing at the beginning of line nine, and often flagged by terms such as "yet," "but," and "however." In the Shakespearean sonnet a volta commonly appears at the beginning of the final couplet, at line thirteen.

Works Cited

Auden, W.H. Foreword. *A Change of World*. By Adrienne Rich. New
    Haven: Yale UP, 1951. 7-11. Print.

Avison, Margaret. "July Man." *The Dumbfounding*. New York: Norton,
    1966. 22. Print.

Baldick, Chris. "Concrete Poetry." *Oxford Dictionary of Literary Terms*.
    3rd ed. Oxford: Oxford UP, 2008. 67. Print.

Bernstein, Charles. *Attack of the Difficult Poems: Essays and Inventions*.
    Chicago: U of Chicago P, 2011. Print.

Bissett, Bill, perf. *bp: pushing the boundaries, a process documentary*.
    Dir. Brian Nash. CINéMAT, 1998. Videocassette.

Blake, William. "The Lamb." 1789. Rosengarten and Goldrick-Jones
    155.

————. "The Tyger." 1794. Rosengarten and Goldrick-Jones 157-58.

Bradstreet, Anne. "Prologue." 1650. *Poetry Foundation*. Web. 8 March
    2014.

Brand, Dionne. "Blues Spiritual for Mammy Prater." 1990. *No
    Language Is Neutral*. Toronto: McClelland & Stewart, 1998. 14-16.
    Print.

Brontë, Charlotte. "Biographical Notice of Ellis and Acton Bell." *Life
    and Works of Charlotte Brontë and Her Sisters*. London: Smith,
    Elder, 1973. ix-xvi. *Google Books*. Web. 21 March 2014.

Brooks, Cleanth. *The Well Wrought Urn: Studies in the Structure of
    Poetry*. New York: Harcourt, Brace & World, 1947. Print.

Brooks, Gwendolyn. "kitchenette building." *Blacks*. Chicago: Third
    World P, 1945. 20. Print.

————. "We Real Cool." 1959. *Selected Poems*. New York: Harper & Row.
    1963. 73. Print.

Brossard, Nicole. "Delirious Coherence." Interview by Susan
    Holbrook. *The Capilano Review* 3.19 (Winter 2013): 5-14. Print.

Cabri, Louis. "Ravine." *Posh Lust*. Vancouver: New Star, 2014. 56. Print.

Carroll, Lewis. "Jabberwocky." 1871. *Through the Looking-Glass. Project Gutenberg eBook*. Web. 27 July 2014.

Christakos, Margaret. "Late One Night." *Multitudes*. Toronto: Coach House P, 2013. 38. Print.

_____. "Love Song." *Multitudes*. Toronto: Coach House P, 2013. 17. Print.

Clifton, Lucille. "at the cemetery, walnut grove plantation, south Carolina, 1989." *quilting: poems, 1987-1990*. Brockport, NY: BOA Editions, 1991. 11-12. Print.

Corner, John. *Pictographs (Indian Rock Paintings) in the Interior of British Columbia*. Vernon, BC: Wayside P, 1968. Print.

Cullen, Countee. "Tableau." 1925. *Voices from the Harlem Renaissance*. Ed. Nathan Irvin Huggins. New York: Oxford UP, 1976. 145-46. Print.

Cummings, E.E. "l(a." 1958. *95 Poems*. New York: Liveright, 2002. 1. Print.

_____. "r-p-o-p-h-e-s-s-a-g-r". 1932. *Selected Poems*. Ed. Richard S. Kennedy. New York: Liveright, 1994. 42. Print.

_____. "since feeling is first." 1926. *E.E. Cummings: Complete Poems 1914-1962*. Ed. George J. Firmage, New York: Liveright, 1991. 291. Print.

Dickinson, Emily. "A narrow Fellow in the Grass." 1866. *The Complete Poems of Emily Dickinson*. Ed. Thomas H. Johnson. Boston: Little, Brown, 1960. 459-60. Print.

Dijkstra, Bram. *Hieroglyphics of a New Speech: Cubism, Stieglitz, and the Early Poetry of William Carlos Williams*. Princeton: Princeton UP, 1969. Print.

Dilworth, Thomas. "Beauty and Truth: The Shakespearean Proto-Text for Keats's 'Grecian Urn'." *PLL* 51.1 (2015): 51-59. Print.

Donne, John. "The Flea." 1633. Rosengarten and Goldrick-Jones 41-42.

Doolittle, Hilda ("H.D."). "Sheltered Garden." *Sea Garden*. London: Constable, 1916. 18-19. *Project Gutenberg eBook*. Web. 8 March 2014.

Dutton, Paul. "so'net 1." *Right Hemisphere, Left Ear*. Toronto: Coach House P, 1979. Print.

Evans, Blakemore, ed. *The Sonnets*. Cambridge: Cambridge UP, 1996. Print.

Furniss, Tom, and Michael Bath. *Reading Poetry: An Introduction*. 2nd ed. Harlow, UK: Pearson, 2007. Print.

Ginsberg, Allen. "A Supermarket in California." *Howl and Other Poems*. San Francisco: City Lights Books, 1956. 29-30. Print.

Gordimer, Nadine. Back cover blurb for *Dark Fields of the Republic: Poems, 1991-1995*. By Adrienne Rich. New York: W.W. Norton, 1995.

Gottschall, Jonathan. *The Storytelling Animal: How Stories Make Us Human*. Boston: Houghton Mifflin Harcourt, 2012. Print.

Halfe, Louise Bernice. "Body Politics." *Bear Bones & Feathers*. Regina, SK: Coteau Books, 1994. 32. Print.

Heaney, Seamus. Interview by Eleanor Wachtel. *Writers and Company*. CBC. 23 May 2010. Radio.

Hemingway, Ernest. *Ballantine Ale* advertisement. *Life* 33 (8 September 1952): 56-57. Print.

Herbert, George. "Easter Wings." 1633. *Metaphysical Lyrics & Poems of the 17th Century*. Ed. Herbert J.C. Grierson. Oxford: Clarendon, 1921. 104. *Internet Archive*. Web. 7 January 2014.

Hopkins, Gerard Manley. "God's Grandeur." 1918. Rosengarten and Goldrick-Jones 348.

Hughes, Langston. "The Weary Blues." 1925. *Poetry Foundation*. Web. 25 September 2013.

Johnson, James Weldon. Preface. *The Book of American Negro Poetry*. Ed. James Weldon Johnson. New York: Harcourt, Brace, 1922. 5-22. *Project Gutenberg eBook*. Web. 24 September 2013.

Keats, John. *Letters of John Keats to His Family and Friends*. Ed. Sidney Colvin. London: MacMillan, 1891. *Project Gutenberg eBook*. Web. 15 November 2013.

———. "Ode on a Grecian Urn." 1820. *Keats: Poems Published in 1820*. Ed. M. Robertson. Oxford: Clarendon, 1909. 113-16. *Project Gutenberg eBook*. Web. 25 October 2013.

____. "Ode to a Nightingale." 1820. *The Poetical Works of John Keats.*
Ed. Francis T. Palgrave. London: MacMillan, 1884. 213-15.
Bartleby.com. Web. 25 October 2013.

Koch, Kenneth. "To My Twenties." *New Addresses.* New York: Alfred
A. Knopf, 2000. 18-19. Print.

Langdell, Cheri Colby. *Adrienne Rich: The Moment of Change.*
Westport, CT: Praeger-Greenwood, 2004. Print.

Library of America. *American Poetry: The Twentieth Century.* Vol. 1.
New York, 2000. Print.

Livesay, Dorothy. "The Three Emilys." 1953. *The Self-Completing Tree.*
Vancouver: Beach Holme Publishing, 1999. 83. Print.

Lowell, Amy. "Venus Transiens." 1915. Library of America 168-69.

McFee, Michael. "In Medias Res." *Colander.* Pittsburgh: Carnegie
Mellon UP, 1996. 51. Print.

McKay, Claude. "The Castaways." *Spring in New Hampshire* 28.

____. "The Harlem Dancer." *Spring in New Hampshire* 33.

____. *Harlem Shadows.* New York: Harcourt, Brace, 1922. *Internet
Archive.* Web. 23 September 2013.

____. *Spring in New Hampshire and Other Poems.* London: Grant
Richards, 1920. *Internet Archive.* Web. 23 September 2013.

Millay, Edna St. Vincent. "I, being born a woman and distressed."
1923. Library of America 863-64.

Miner, Paul. "'The Tyger': Genesis & Evolution in the Poetry of
William Blake." *Criticism* 4.1 (Winter 1962): 59-73. *JSTOR.* Web.
20 November 2013.

Moore, Clement C. "A Visit From St. Nicholas." *Poems.* New York:
Bartlett & Welford, 1844. 124-27. Print.

Moore, Marianne. "Bird-Witted." 1936. *The Complete Poems of
Marianne Moore.* New York: Viking, 1967. 105-06. Print.

Mouré, Erin. "Rolling Motion." *Furious.* Toronto: House of Anansi,
1988. 35. Print.

Mullen, Harryette. "Dim Lady." *Sleeping with the Dictionary.* Berkeley
and Los Angeles: U of California P, 2002. 20. Print.

Nichol, bp. "Cycle No. 22." *As Elected: Selected Writing 1962-1979.* Ed.
bp Nichol and Jack David. Vancouver: Talonbooks, 1980. 49.
Print.

_____. *Love: a book of remembrances*. Vancouver: Talonbooks, 1974. Print.

Notley, Alice. "Sonnet 15." *165 Meeting House Lane*. New York: C Press, 1971. Print.

Nourai, Ali. *An Etymological Dictionary of Persian, English and Other Indo-European Languages*. *Xlibris*. Web. 3 September 2013.

O'Hara, Frank. "Why I Am Not a Painter." 1957. *The Collected Poems of Frank O'Hara*. Berkeley and Los Angeles: U of California P, 1971. 261. Print.

Padgett, Ron. "Nothing in That Drawer." *Great Balls of Fire*. 1969. Minneapolis, MN: Coffee House P, 1990. 5. Print.

Perloff, Marjorie. "The Two Ariels: The (Re)making of the Sylvia Plath Canon." *The American Poetry Review* 13.6 (1984): 10-18. *JSTOR*. Web. 22 February 2014.

Philip, Marlene Nourbese. "*Zong!* #1." *Zong!* Middletown, CT: Wesleyan UP, 2008. 3-4. Print.

Plath, Sylvia. "Daddy." *Ariel*. New York: Harper & Row, 1965. 49-51. Print.

_____. "Appendix II: Script for the BBC Broadcast 'New Poems by Sylvia Plath.'" *Ariel: The Restored Edition*. New York: Harper Perennial, 2004. 195-97. Print.

Plotkin, Wendy. "kitchenettes." *The Electronic Encyclopedia of Chicago*. Chicago Historical Society, 2005. Web. 28 February 2014.

Pope, Alexander. "An Essay on Criticism." *The Major Works*. Ed. Pat Rogers. New York: Oxford UP, 2006. 17-39. Print.

Pound, Ezra. "A Retrospect." 1918. *The Poetics of the New American Poetry*. Ed. Donald Allen and Warren Tallman. New York: Grove P, 1973. 36-48. Print.

_____. "In a Station of the Metro." Library of America 514.

Pratt, E.J. "The Shark." *The Collected Works of E.J. Pratt*. Ed. Sandra Djwa and R.G. Moyles. Toronto: U of Toronto P, 1989. 66-67. Print.

Quartermain, Peter, ed. *Dictionary of Literary Biography*, Vol. 45: American Poets 1880-1945. Detroit: Gale Research, 1986. Print.

Rich, Adrienne. "Aunt Jennifer's Tigers." *A Change of World*. New Haven: Yale UP, 1951. 19. Print.

_____. Interview. *The Language of Life: A Festival of Poets*. By Bill
    Moyers. New York: Broadway Books, 1995. 335-53. Print.

_____. "When We Dead Awaken: Writing as Re-Vision (1971)." *On Lies,
    Secrets, and Silence: Selected Prose 1966-1978*. New York: W.W.
    Norton, 1979. 33-50. Print.

Robertson, Lisa. "monday." *the weather*. Vancouver: New Star Books,
    2001. 9-12. Print.

Rose, Jacqueline. *The Haunting of Sylvia Plath*. Cambridge, MA:
    Harvard UP, 1992. Print.

Rosengarten, Herbert and Amanda Goldrick-Jones, eds. *The
    Broadview Anthology of Poetry*. Peterborough, ON: Broadview P,
    1993. Print.

Rosenthal, M.L. "Poetry as Confession." *Our Life in Poetry*. New York:
    Persea Books, 1991. 109-13. Print.

Rossetti, Christina. "In an Artist's Studio." 1896. *Selected Poems of
    Christina Rossetti*. Ware: Bibliophile Books, 1994. 5. Print.

Shakespeare, William. Sonnet 18. Evans 41.

_____. Sonnet 20. Evans 42.

_____. Sonnet 73. Evans 69.

_____. Sonnet 116. Evans 90.

_____. Sonnet 130. Evans 97.

Shelley, Percy Bysshe. *A Defence of Poetry*. Ed. Albert S. Cook. Boston:
    Ginn, 1891. 1-48. *Google Book Search*. Web. 11 September 2013.

Solt, Mary Ellen. "Forsythia." *Flowers in Concrete*. Bloomington,
    IN: Fine Arts Department, Indiana U, 1966. *UbuWeb*. Web. 2
    January 2014.

Spencer, Anne. "Letter to My Sister." *Ebony and Topaz: A Collectanea*.
    Ed. Charles S. Johnson. New York: National Urban League, 1927.
    94. Print.

Stein, Gertrude. "ASPARAGUS." *Tender Buttons*. 1914. Mineola, NY:
    Dover, 1997. 33. Print.

_____. "A DOG." *Tender Buttons*. 1914. Mineola, NY: Dover, 1997. 16.
    Print.

_____. "Preciosilla." 1926. *Selected Writings of Gertrude Stein*. Ed. Carl
    Van Vechten. New York: Random House, 1946. 550-51. Print.

Steiner, George. "Dying is an Art." *The Art of Sylvia Plath: A Symposium*. Ed. Charles Newman. London: Faber and Faber, 1970. 211-18. Print.

Truscott, Mark. "Winter." *Said Like Reeds or Things*. Toronto: Coach House, 2004. 27. Print.

Wah, Fred. "nvsble trck." *Pictograms from the Interior of B.C.* Vancouver: Talonbooks, 1975. 24-25. Print.

——. Interview. "A Conversation with Fred Wah and Pauline Butling." By bp Nichol. *Open Letter* 3.9 (Fall 1978): 34-63. Print.

Webb, Phyllis. "Sunday Water: Thirteen Anti-Ghazals." *Water and Light: Ghazals and Anti-Ghazals*. Toronto: Coach House P, 1984. 7-21. Print.

——. "Poetics Against the Angel of Death." *The Sea Is Also a Garden*. Toronto: Ryerson P, 1962. 39. Print.

Wershler-Henry, Darren. "Sonnet for Bonnie." *Nicholodeon*. Toronto: Coach House P, 1997. Unpag. Print.

Whitman, Walt. "When I Heard the Learn'd Astronomer." 1865. *Walt Whitman: The Complete Poems*. London: Penguin, 1975. 298. Print.

Williams, Hywel. *Cassell's Chronology of World History*. London: Weidenfeld & Nicolson, 2005. Print.

Williams, Neville. *Chronology of the Modern World: 1763 to the Present Time*. New York: D. McKay, 1966. Print.

Williams, William Carlos. "The Dance." 1944. *The Collected Poems of William Carlos Williams Vol. II: 1939-1962*. Ed. A. Walton Litz and Christopher MacGowan. New York: New Directions, 1988. 58. Print.

——. "Young Sycamore." 1927. *The Collected Poems of William Carlos Williams Vol. I: 1909-1939*. Ed. A. Walton Litz and Christopher MacGowan. New York: New Directions, 1986. 266. Print.

Wordsworth, William. "I Wandered Lonely as a Cloud." *The Complete Poetical Works*. London: Macmillan, 1888. *Bartleby.com*. Web. 26 July 2014.

——. "Preface to Lyrical Ballads (1800/1802)." *Lyrical Ballads & Other Poems*. By William Wordsworth and Samuel Taylor Coleridge. Ware, UK: Wordsworth Editions, 2003. 5-25. Print.

Permissions
Acknowledgements

Avison, Margaret. "July Man," from *Always Now, Collected Poems of Margaret Avison*. Porcupine's Quill, 2003. Reprinted with the permission of Porcupine's Quill and the Estate of Margaret Avison.

Brand, Dionne. "Blues Spiritual for Mammy Prater," from *No Language is Neutral*. Copyright © 1990 Dionne Brand. Reprinted by permission of McClelland & Stewart, a division of Penguin Random House Canada Limited, a Penguin Random House Company.

Brooks, Gwendolyn. "kitchenette building," from *Blacks*. Chicago: Third World Press, 1945. Reprinted by consent of Brooks Permissions.

Cabri, Louis. "Ravine," from *Posh Lust*. Vancouver: New Star, 2014. Reprinted with the permission of New Star Books.

Christakos, Margaret. "Late One Night" and "Love Song," from *Multitudes*, copyright © Margaret Christakos, 2013. Reprinted with the permission of Coach House Books.

Clifton, Lucille. "at the cemetary, walnut grove plantation, south carolina, 1989," from *The Collected Poems of Lucillle Clifton*. Copyright © 1991 by Lucille Clifton. Reprinted with the permission of The Permissions Company, Inc., on behalf of BOA Editions Ltd., www.boaeditions.org.

Cullen, Countee. "Tableau," 1925, from *Voices from the Harlem Renaissance*, edited by Nathan Irvin Huggins. New York: Oxford University Press, 1976. Originally published in *On These I Stand*, Harper & Brothers, 1947. Reprinted with the permission of the Amistad Research Center, Tulane University.

Cummings, E.E. "l(a," from *95 Poems* by e.e. cummings. New York: Harcourt, Brace & Company, 1950-1958. Copyright © 1958, 1986, 1991 by the Trustees for the E.E. Cummings Trust. "r-p-o-p-h-e-s-s-a-g-r," from *Collected Poems*. New York: Harcourt Brace and Company, 1923-1938. Copyright © 1935, 1963, 1991 by the Trustees for the E.E. Cummings Trust. "since feeling is first," from *is 5*. New York: Horace Liveright, 1926. Copyright © 1926, 1954, 1991 by the Trustees for the E.E. Cummings Trust. Used by permission of Liveright Publishing Corporation.

Dickinson, Emily. "A Narrow Fellow in the Grass," from *The Poems of Emily Dickinson: Variorum Edition*, edited by Ralph W. Franklin, Cambridge, MA: The Belknap Press of Harvard University Press, Copyright © 1998 by the President and Fellows of Harvard College. Copyright © 1951, 1955 by the President and Fellows of Harvard College. Copyright © renewed 1979, 1983 by the President and Fellows of Harvard College. Copyright © 1914, 1918, 1919, 1924, 1929, 1930, 1932, 1935, 1937, 1942 by Martha Dickinson Bianchi. Copyright © 1952, 1957, 1958, 1963, 1965 by Mary L. Hampson. Reprinted by permission of the publishers and the Trustees of Amherst College.

Dutton, Paul. "so'net 1," from *Right Hemisphere, Left Ear*. Copyright © Paul Dutton, 1979. Reprinted with the permission of Coach House Books.

Ginsberg, Allen. "A Supermarket in California," from *Collected Poems 1947-1980*. Copyright © 1955 by Allen Ginsberg. Reprinted by permission of HarperCollins Publishers.

Halfe, Louise. "Body Politics," from the collection *Bear Bones &*

Plath, Sylvia. "Daddy," from *Ariel*. Copyright © 1963 by Ted Hughes. Reprinted by permission of HarperCollins Publishers.

Pound, Ezra. "In a Station of the Metro," from *Personae*, copyright © 1926 by Ezra Pound. Reprinted by permission of New Directions Publishing Corp.

Pratt, E.J. "The Shark," from *The Collected Works of E.J. Pratt*, edited by Sandra Djwa and R.G. Moyles. Copyright © 1989, University of Toronto Press. Reprinted with the permission of the publisher.

Robertson, Lisa. "monday," from *the weather*. Vancouver: New Star Books, 2001. Reprinted with the permission of New Star Books.

Solt, Mary Ellen. "Forsythia," from *Flowers in Concrete*. Copyright © 1966 Mary Ellen Solt. Reprinted with the permission of Susan Solt, Literary Executor for the Estate of Mary Ellen Solt.

Spencer, Anne. "Letter to My Sister," from *Ebony and Topaz: A Collectanea*, edited by Charles S. Johnson. New York: National Urban League, 1927.

Stein, Gertrude. "Preciosilla," from *Selected Writings of Gertrude Stein*, Random House. Reprinted with the permission of the Estate of Gertrude Stein through Literary Executor Mr. Stanford Gann, Jr., Levin & Gann, P.A.

Truscott, Mark. "Winter," from *Said Like Reeds or Things*, copyright © 2004, Mark Truscott. Reprinted with the permission of Coach House Books.

Wah, Fred. "nvsble trck," from *Pictograms from the Interior of B.C.* Vancouver: Talonbooks, 1975. Reprinted with the permission of Talonbooks. Aboriginal pictograph reproduced by John Corner; reprinted with the permission of Gary Corner.

Webb, Phyllis. "Poetics Against the Angel of Death," from *The Sea Is Also a Garden*. Toronto: Ryerson Press, 1962. Reprinted with the permission of Phyllis Webb.

Wershler-Henry, Darren. "Sonnet for Bonnie," from *Nicholodeon*. Copyright © 1997, Darren Wershler-Henry. Reprinted with the permission of Coach House Books.

Williams, William Carlos. "The Dance" from *Selected Poems*, copyright © 1985 by New Directions Publishing Corp. Reprinted by permission of New Directions Publishing Corp. "Young Sycamore," from *The Collected Poems: Volume I, 1909-1939*, copyright © 1938 by New Directions Publishing Corp. Reprinted by permission of New Directions Publishing Corp.

Images:

"4th November 1964: Manuela Vargas at a dress rehearsal for *The Tigress of the Flamenco* given by her company at the Vaudeville Theatre, London." Dennis Oulds / Hulton Archive / Copyright © Getty Images.

"Sardines," 1955, by Michael Goldberg. Oil and adhesive tape on canvas. Gift of Mr. and Mrs. David K. Anderson, Martha Jackson Memorial Collection. Copyright © Michael Goldberg Estate 2015; courtesy of Michael Rosenfeld Gallery LLC, New York, NY. Photo: Smithsonian American Art Museum, Washington, DC / Art Resource, NY.

"What immortal hand or eye could frame thy fearful symmetry?" Mick Stevens, The New Yorker Collection / The Cartoon Bank.

Index

From the Publisher

A name never says it all, but the word "Broadview" expresses a good deal of the philosophy behind our company. We are open to a broad range of academic approaches and political viewpoints. We pay attention to the broad impact book publishing and book printing has in the wider world; for some years now we have used 100% recycled paper for most titles. Our publishing program is internationally oriented and broad-ranging. Our individual titles often appeal to a broad readership too; many are of interest as much to general readers as to academics and students.

Founded in 1985, Broadview remains a fully independent company owned by its shareholders—not an imprint or subsidiary of a larger multinational.

For the most accurate information on our books (including information on pricing, editions, and formats) please visit our website at www.broadviewpress.com. Our print books and ebooks are also available for sale on our site.

broadview press
www.broadviewpress.com

The interior of this book is printed on 100% recycled paper.

PERMANENT   100%   BIO GAS® ENERGY   Ancient Forest Friendly™